USBORNE

UNDERSTANDING

BUSINESS

Written by
Lara Bryan and
Rose Hall

Illustrated by
Kellan Stover

Business experts:
Wilson Turkington
and Bryony Henry

Contents

Chapter 1: How to start a business

Do you want to start a business? Here are the basics you need to get started: thinking up business ideas, testing them, sussing out your competition, and raising the money you need to start.

Chapter 2: How to sell your stuff

Raring to go? Now you need to answer these questions: where should your goods or services be on sale? How much should you charge? And how do you persuade people to buy them?

Chapter 3: Keeping track of money

How do businesses make sure they spend less money than they make? Why do you need to pay taxes? And why do some businesses fail?

Chapter 4: People in business

Here's where to find out who does what in business. Read about what makes a good leader, how leaders get the best out of their employees, and how businesses can affect consumers and communities.

Chapter 5: Making a product
How do you make something that is high quality, without it costing too much? How do businesses satisfy customers and protect the environment at the same time?

Chapter 6: Growing the business
Bigger is better, isn't it? But how do you grow your business? And can a business ever get *too big*?

Chapter 7: The bigger picture
All businesses are affected by the world around them. Find out about the economy and interest rates and how they affect business. Discover how governments support and control businesses, and the impact of new technology.

I don't think I'm the type of person who goes into business.

Anyone can run a business – there's no such thing as the right type of person to do it!

I'd like to run my own business, but I don't know where to begin!

Well, read on! You'll find out how businesses work. And by the end of Chapter 3, I think you'll have the confidence to start one yourself.

What is a business?

Whether it's one person running a market stall or a big, well-known company with thousands of people working for it, all businesses make and do things people need, in exchange for something – usually money.

   To be successful, a business has to make more money than it spends. This is known as making a **profit**.

A business might be...

...a farm.

EGGS

...a store on a street.

PHARMACY

Hotel

TOWN BANK

We sell medicines.

We keep our customers' money safe.

...a website.

BUYSHOES.COM

...a big office.

40,000 people work for this airline company. We're a **large** business.

The shoes of your dreams!

...an oil well.

...a factory.

There are 700 of us working in this factory. We're **a medium-sized business**.

...a market stall.

My business has just one worker – me!

...a car.

Most businesses, like my taxi service, employ fewer than ten employees.

We're known as **micro-businesses**.

What do businesses do?

Businesses make products and sell them. A product can be something you hold, such as a book or a stuffed toy. This is known as a **good**.

Can I have a stuffed bear?

$5.99

A product can also be an action, such as delivering groceries or cutting someone's hair. This is known as a **service**.

It's time for a haircut!

Some businesses offer products that are a mixture of goods *and* services.

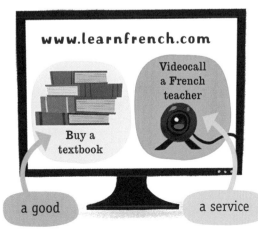

www.learnfrench.com

Videocall a French teacher

Buy a textbook

a good

a service

Why do we need businesses?

Imagine a world without businesses. You'd have to make or get everything you needed by yourself – and everyone else would too.

Here's an example of a need: a chocolate cake.

> You don't *need* cake! You need a winter coat.

> It's still called a "need" even if it's just something you *want* to have.

Most people can imagine baking a cake by themselves.

Ingredients

Eggs
Flour
Butter
Chocolate

But imagine having to make and grow all the ingredients as well. You'd have to...

...grind cocoa beans to make chocolate.

...churn milk into butter.

...find a hen and collect its eggs.

...plant wheat and mill it into flour.

Mmm, this might take a while.

Splitting work is a more effective way of satisfying people's needs. An individual person, or group of people, can specialize in the things they are good at, and turn those into **businesses**.

I grow wheat on my farm and sell it to a flour mill.

We produce chocolate and sell it to stores.

The milk from my cows is sold in local convenience stores.

Each person sells their goods or services, and uses the money to buy *other* things they need.

I get paid to install ovens into people's homes.

I make money from writing recipe books.

I couldn't have made my cake without all those businesses.

And now I could even start *my own* business making and selling cakes. Then I could use the money I make to buy a winter coat.

Business is everywhere

Here are some examples of the range of needs that people have, and the kinds of businesses – and business people – that meet them.

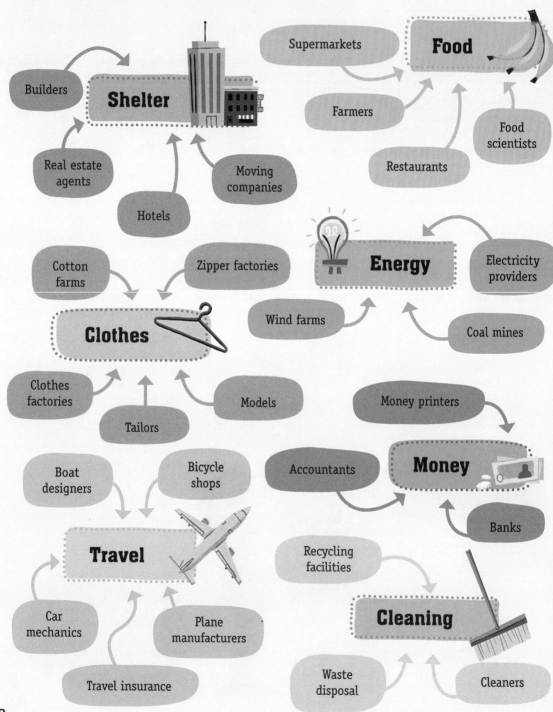

Builders

Shelter

Supermarkets

Food

Real estate agents

Farmers

Moving companies

Food scientists

Hotels

Restaurants

Cotton farms

Zipper factories

Energy

Electricity providers

Clothes

Wind farms

Coal mines

Clothes factories

Models

Money printers

Tailors

Boat designers

Bicycle shops

Accountants

Money

Banks

Travel

Recycling facilities

Car mechanics

Plane manufacturers

Cleaning

Travel insurance

Waste disposal

Cleaners

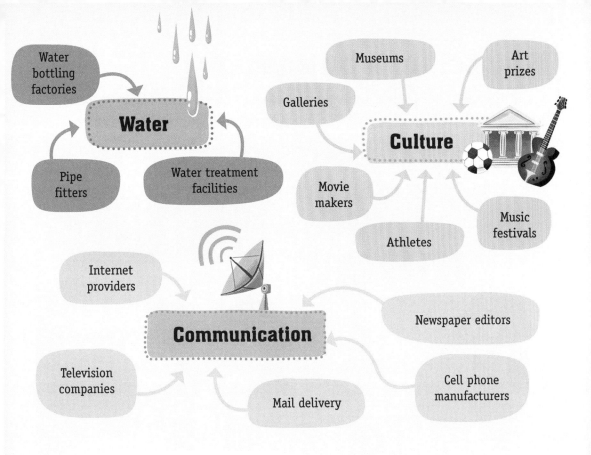

...but not quite everywhere

Some goods and services are provided by *governments* instead of businesses. This might be because the government has decided to make something available to everyone – whether they can pay for it or not – such as healthcare, education or street maintenance.

Could I get clothes for free?

No, but some other things *are* most often free.

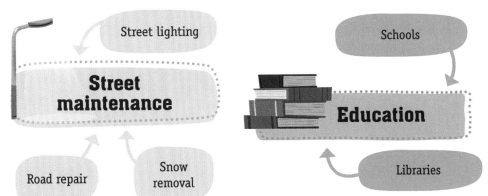

Street lighting

Street maintenance

Road repair

Snow removal

Schools

Education

Libraries

Why set up a business?

Someone who sets up a business is often called an **entrepreneur**. There are all kinds of reasons why people become entrepreneurs.

Some people do it to make money...

Sometimes, someone spots a problem, and wants to fix it...

Some people start a business to make the world a better place...

Whenever you see this symbol, it means the example is about a real business.

Some entrepreneurs get a buzz from turning ideas into products...

Entrepreneurs tend to start businesses for a combination of these reasons. They often get huge satisfaction from offering the best possible product or service.

Chapter 1:
How to start a business

Do **you** want to be an entrepreneur? You can be. Absolutely anyone can start their own business. All you need to do is think it through a little. The next chapter will show you how.

First you need to come up with an **idea**.

Next, you have to test it. This is to make sure there is a **market** for your good or service, and that it will stand out against the **competition**.

Then, you can create a **business plan** to help you set your goals and persuade people to support you.

Your idea

All businesses start with an idea. If nothing comes to mind right away, you could try making a "mind map" to help you. To do that, write these questions in bubbles on a sheet of paper, then scribble as many ideas you can think of around each one.

What am I good at that someone might pay me for?

Playing the piano... could I perform at weddings?

Card tricks... people could hire me for parties?

What am I doing already that I could convince people to pay me for?

Dogwalking

Washing cars

Giving people advice... could I be a life coach?

How could I combine my skills with someone else's to make a fantastic product or service?

My sister has a car and I make tasty pastries... pastry delivery company?

My friend can draw and I'm good with computers... designing and printing greeting cards?

After you've finished your mind map, read it through carefully and pick out the business ideas you like the most.

If you have come up with some promising ideas, the next step is to find out whether anyone will *actually buy* the things you want to sell. It's also useful to work out whether you will be *competing* with existing businesses.

Does anyone want your stuff?

Even if you know that *you* would buy a good or service, it's important to find out if anyone else would be willing to pay for it.

I'm Nathan. I love spicy food and I love popcorn.

So I've decided to make my own 'SpiceCorn' to sell at school. You can't get spicy popcorn nearby.

spice mix

Every kid will want to buy a box of SpiceCorn! I'm going to make so much money!

Ugh, gross! What's that weird taste?

Do you have any normal popcorn?

Aagh! It's too hot!

Oh no! Look at all these boxes I have left over. I've lost so much money.

To avoid wasting money developing products or services that no one wants, businesses do **market research**. This means talking to the group of people you hope will become customers – your **market**.

Businesses define their market by grouping people together that have something in common. For example, they might aim their goods or services at people who live in one specific place, or are of a particular age, or who have a similar income, or who share a hobby.

I'm a financial advisor in Tokyo and my market is extremely rich people in Japan.

Nathan's market is students at his school, so these are the people that he needs to research. He does this in a number of ways.

Observations

I have counted 32 kids who bought popcorn after school at the local store. That shows it *is* popular.

Interviews

How much would you be willing to pay for a box of popcorn this size?

Would you like to buy a snack at break time?

It's better to ask questions that people can answer however they like. If you ask a question such as, "do you like my idea?" they might just say, "yes" to make you feel good.

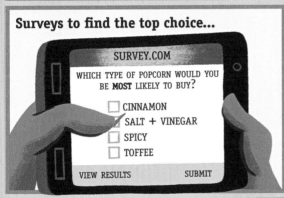

Surveys to find the top choice...

SURVEY.COM

WHICH TYPE OF POPCORN WOULD YOU BE **MOST** LIKELY TO BUY?

☐ CINNAMON
☐ SALT + VINEGAR
☐ SPICY
☐ TOFFEE

VIEW RESULTS   SUBMIT

...and bottom choice

SURVEY.COM
RESULTS
WHICH TYPE OF POPCORN WOULD YOU BE *LEAST* LIKELY TO BUY?

SPICY
CINAMMON
SALT+VINEGAR
TOFFEE

Oh dear! No one wants the spicy flavor!

Testing sessions

Please could you taste them and tell me which one you like best?

These are four different recipes for salt and vinegar popcorn.

Do you have suggestions for improvements?

The more research, the better

The more people you ask from within your market, the more useful the information you gather will be. Market research takes time, but it allows you to develop a good or service that is just what your customers want. This makes it much easier to persuade people to buy it.

Be the best!

Rivalry between businesses for customers is called **competition**. Competition can come from different places. For example, if Martha starts a business selling T-shirts at the Saturday market in her town, she may have several competitors. Here are some of them.

Ways to get ahead

In order to get ahead of the competition, businesses try to be better than their rivals in one or more ways.

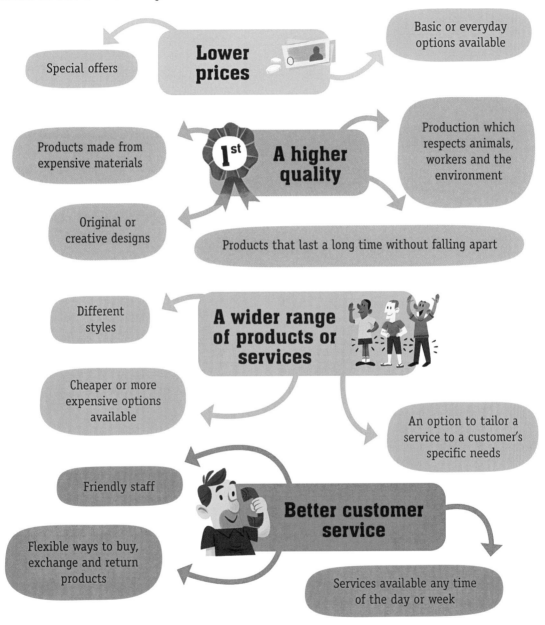

Special offers

Lower prices

Basic or everyday options available

Products made from expensive materials

1st A higher quality

Production which respects animals, workers and the environment

Original or creative designs

Products that last a long time without falling apart

Different styles

A wider range of products or services

Cheaper or more expensive options available

An option to tailor a service to a customer's specific needs

Friendly staff

Better customer service

Flexible ways to buy, exchange and return products

Services available any time of the day or week

Healthy competition

From a customer's point of view, competition is a good thing, because it can push businesses to offer better products at lower prices. Most countries have laws to *ensure* businesses compete. For example, it's illegal in many places for businesses to agree among themselves to set a fixed price.

How to beat the competition

To win customers, you either need to be first on the scene with a good or service, or to offer something better than your rivals. This flowchart could help you work out how.

Is another business already selling what you want to sell?

NO   **YES**

Does your market research definitely show that customers need or want your new product or service?

YES   **NO**

If no one wants it, that explains why there is no competition! Think of a new idea instead.

You should try to make your product or service stand out from the competition.

Higher quality
Google™ wasn't the first internet search engine. In 1998, the market was dominated by other businesses. *Google* soon took over the market because their search gave more useful results.

REAL EXAMPLE

REAL EXAMPLE

New features
Mp3 players already existed when *Apple* launched the iPod ®. But iPods were the first to come with software – iTunes ® – to organize and transfer music more easily.

If you are the first to sell an exciting new good or service, you have an advantage. Even if competing businesses start up, your customers may stick with you because they know and like you.

REAL EXAMPLE

First
Amazon was the first ever online bookstore. While their customer base has increased they still have to improve their services constantly to keep their large share of the market.

Find the gap in a crowded market

If you have lots of competitors, it can be hard to get your product noticed. So it helps to find a "gap in the market", which means something that isn't currently on offer. To do this, you could draw a **market map**, a diagram which arranges existing products, according to their key characteristics.

Sondhya is considering setting up a business selling sunglasses and she's looking for a gap in the market. So she's drawn a market map showing all the sunglasses that are already on sale in her town.

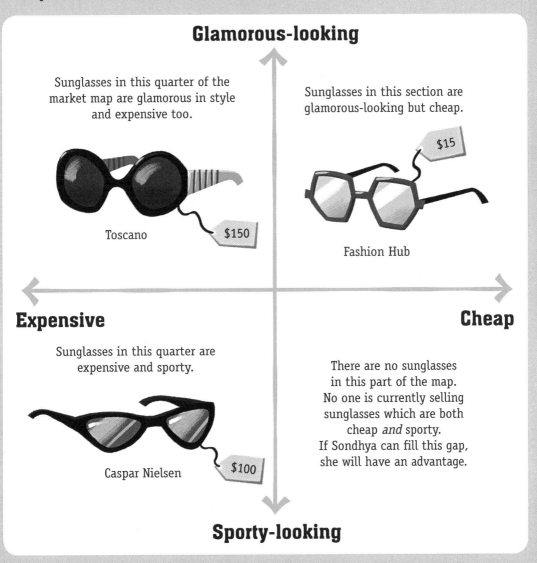

Glamorous-looking

Sunglasses in this quarter of the market map are glamorous in style and expensive too.

Sunglasses in this section are glamorous-looking but cheap.

$15

Toscano $150

Fashion Hub

Expensive   **Cheap**

Sunglasses in this quarter are expensive and sporty.

There are no sunglasses in this part of the map. No one is currently selling sunglasses which are both cheap *and* sporty. If Sondhya can fill this gap, she will have an advantage.

Caspar Nielsen $100

Sporty-looking

You could make a market map for any product, showing any of its features. For example, you could compare snack bars by mapping the age of the product's target customers on one scale, and how healthy it is on the other scale.

Need money?

Most businesses need *some* money to get started – whether to pay wages, buy equipment, rent a space or pay for advertising. It's often called **startup capital**.

How can I pay a computer coder to help me get my memory training app started?

Apply for a grant

A grant is a gift of money. A government may make grants available for businesses that meet certain criteria, such as being a new business – called a startup.

Save

Savings can help you get started. But if the business fails, you won't get the money back.

Apply for a loan

Family, friends or the bank might lend you money. But you'll probably have to pay back a bit more than you borrowed. The extra amount is known as **interest** – find out more on page 116.

Crowdfund

This means asking a very large group of people to pay a little bit of money each, often through a specialized website. In return, each person gets a small gift or reward.

Find investors

Investors are people who offer money in exchange for owning part of the company. Choose carefully! They'll expect to have a say in the business and hope to make money by selling their share later on.

Top tips

New businesses often find it tricky to raise money. That's because there is always a risk that the business will fail and not be able to pay the money back. To be taken seriously, here are some things to think about doing:

1. If you're borrowing money from friends or family, draw up a written agreement to avoid misunderstandings later on.

Agreement of loan

2. Consider how much money you need. Don't spend too much at the beginning, and make sure you only get things you really need.

TO GET

bodyguard

phone line

limousine

chef to cook lunch

stationery

You may need more money than you originally thought, so plan for that too.

3. Make a **business plan** – a booklet that describes your business and how it will make money and achieve its goals. It sounds boring but it's important – it will show that you've thought things through, and help you win other people's support.

Our band is called **THE ROCKETTS** and we need to borrow some money for recording equipment.

We've made a business plan. That doesn't sound very rock 'n' roll – but it will convince people to help us!

Turn the page to see our plan for success.

BUSINESS PLAN

The roadmap to music stardom

These are the kinds of questions you need to answer in your business plan.

Business plan

Introduction

We're THE ROCKETTS – three cousins in a band from Montreal, Canada. We write all our own music, and already have a growing fan base.

THE ROCKETTS

Describe your business. What's so special about it?

Business goals

Play four concerts this summer, get 50 new people to subscribe to our YouTube channel every month, record an album, and generate enough money from selling tickets and albums to start making a profit.

Picking specific goals makes it easier to measure your progress.

Competitors

Our competitors are local bands, such as XYZ and Mashup. They tend to sell their concert tickets for C$5. But we're more popular than they are – we have more subscribers on YouTube.

Who else is selling what you are? How much do they charge? What makes your product better?

C$ means "Canadian dollars" – the money people use in Canada.

What to do with your plan

First of all, get someone to look through the plan to make sure there aren't any mistakes and that you haven't left anything out. Then make several copies to hand out.

Use your plan to try to convince people to support you with money, resources or good advice.

You could add in some numbers to help prove how popular you are. How many subscribers do you have on your YouTube channel?

We've got 300 subscribers.

Customers

Our fans are high-school students and some of their parents. They like us because we are fun, creative and cousins – it makes for a good story! They find out about us through word of mouth, posters in schools and our YouTube channel.

Who are your customers and why will they like your product? How will they find out about it?

What you need

We need to raise money to rent professional recording equipment and to pay for transportation to concert venues. So we need about C$200 to go to the next level.

Do you need any training, equipment, materials or a location to get started? How much will those things cost?

Making money

We'll charge C$5 for concert tickets. We estimate it will take about four months to pay back the C$200. From then on we hope to be making about C$100 per month as a band.

How much will you charge for the product? How much money do you expect to make? (See more on pages 34 and 54.)

Make it official

It's worth finding out whether there are rules about doing business in the place you live. You may need to register your business with the government, or get permission to sell things in a specific location.

Getting permission

Wherever you're planning to sell, think about who you might need to ask.

Want to sell popcorn at school?	Want to run a lemonade stand in the town square? 

Ask a teacher.

Check with city officials.

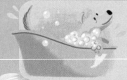 Want to offer a dog-grooming service at a festival?

Ask the festival organizers first.

Telling the government

Businesses usually have to register with the government. You have to choose a type of business, or **structure**, when you register. The simplest one is called a **sole proprietor**.

Just one person in charge

SOLE PROPRIETOR

Minimal paperwork

Usually the only structure allowed if you're under 18

The owner can keep all the profits (minus any **taxes** they need to pay - see below).

Businesses have to pay money to the government, known as **taxes**. Be sure to check with your city and state tax agencies to learn how to pay your taxes. See more on taxes on page 58.

Taking on responsibility

Most businesses are sole proprietors and many are successful. But one downside is that sole proprietors are entirely responsible, or **liable**, for trying to pay back any money their business loses. This is called **unlimited liability**.

I'm a sole proprietor and my construction business has gone under!

To pay back all the money that I borrowed, I need to sell my house and car.

Some business structures protect against this risk. The most common one is called a **limited liability company** (or **LLC**). Business with this structure have **limited liability**, which means the owners are only partly responsible for any money lost.

It's a shame that our business didn't work out, but what a relief we became a limited liability company.

We need to sell the business's assets, but at least our personal possessions are safe!

In most countries, the ownership of a limited company is split up into equal parts, called **shares**, owned by **shareholders**. Profits from the business are shared between the shareholders. Find out more on page 102.

Other types of business

Partnership – similar to being a sole proprietor, but business decisions and profits are shared with a partner or partners.

Cooperative – owned and run by its members, which could mean every single person working there. Profits are shared between the members.

Franchise – this is where you pay an existing business to use their idea. It's less risky because the idea has already been shown to work.

Not-for-profit – any money it makes is used to help people in need. This kind of business is usually a charity or a school.

Doing the right thing

Just like individual people, businesses are supposed to act honestly, fairly and with respect for people and the environment. This is known as behaving **ethically**. To make sure a business is ethical, here are some things entrepreneurs need to think about.

> **How does my business impact on...**

> **...my staff?**
>
> How will I treat the people who work for my company?

> **...the environment?**
>
> How much water and electricity am I using? How am I transporting my products to customers? See more on page 93.

> **...communities?**
>
> How does my business affect people living nearby? My local town? The world? See more on pages 80-81.

> **...customers?**
>
> How does my product change customers' lives? Is it in a good way?

If it's legal, is it OK?

A country's laws send a signal to businesses about what's right and wrong. Some businesses make money doing things that are legal, but that many people think are unethical, such as selling cigarettes. What do you think?

> Our company makes and sells cigarettes. Would you like some?

> Scientists and doctors have proved that they are bad for people. So why are you selling cigarettes to me?

> Because you *want* them don't you? And businesses provide things that people want.

> So if I wanted a *bomb*, would you sell it to me?

> No, because that would be against the law! Cigarettes are unhealthy, but *not* illegal.

Crossing the line

The difficulty with just sticking to the law is that it can't cover every situation. What's more, the line between what's legal and what's illegal isn't always clear. It's sometimes more useful to think about whether or not something seems *fair*.

Ethics isn't just about what a business *does*, either – it's also about how people within a business *behave*. Do you think this manager has crossed a line?

Good ethics is good business

Often, getting managers to behave fairly encourages all staff to work well. When people are calm and happy, they tend to work better, and in turn make more money for the business. So good ethics go hand in hand with good business practice.

Chapter 2:
How to sell your stuff

Once you have a great idea, you need to know how to sell it! Ways to persuade customers to buy your good or service are known as **marketing**. Clever marketing will ensure that customers want your product and buy it from *you* and not your competitors.

Giving your business an appealing personality, or **brand**, helps to make customers connect with your business emotionally. Deciding the **price** of your product, where it will be sold and how to **promote** it is also essential.

Where can customers buy it?

Customers are more likely to buy a product if it is on sale somewhere convenient. To help decide *where* to sell, a business has to think about where its customers go and how they like to buy things.

Imagine a business selling a lunchbox called 'Lunchpax'. A potential customer is someone with an office job, who might take a packed lunch to work. Here are some places the business could sell them Lunchpax, in an average day.

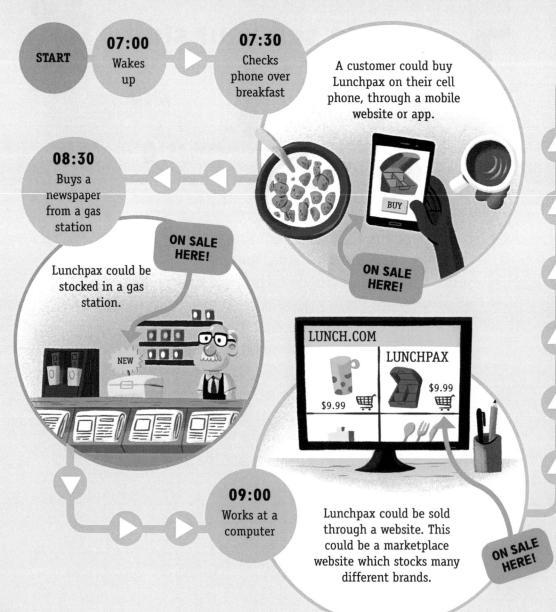

START

07:00 Wakes up

07:30 Checks phone over breakfast

A customer could buy Lunchpax on their cell phone, through a mobile website or app.

BUY

ON SALE HERE!

08:30 Buys a newspaper from a gas station

ON SALE HERE!

Lunchpax could be stocked in a gas station.

NEW

LUNCH.COM

LUNCHPAX

$9.99

$9.99

09:00 Works at a computer

Lunchpax could be sold through a website. This could be a marketplace website which stocks many different brands.

ON SALE HERE!

SUPER-MART

LUNCHPAX!
BUY
BUY
BUY

BUY
BUY
BUY

NEW!

Lunchpax could be on sale at a supermarket.

17:00

Goes to a supermarket after work

ON SALE HERE!

ON SALE HERE!

18:00

Arrives home

The business could sell Lunchpax directly to customers by knocking on doors with samples. It's good to pick a time that lots of people are likely to be at home.

NEW!
Multi-compartment
LUNCHPAX

ORDER NOW!!!
1-800-555-5555

Lunchpax could be sold through a catalog. Catalogs can be delivered to customers, then customers call up or mail a form back to order products.

19:00

Opens mail

ON SALE HERE!

ON SALE HERE!

LUNCH PAX!

20:00

Visits a neighbor for dinner.

The business could recruit people to sell Lunchpax to friends and neighbors. This is called a "party" model of selling. The seller invites neighbors to their home and combines socializing with selling a product.

22:30

Bedtime

FINISH

After selling your product in several places, you can choose the ones which work best and concentrate on them.

What's it worth?

Your good or service is only *worth* what customers are willing to pay. If your price is too high, customers will be put off. If the price is too low, you won't make any money (and you may even lose money).

Price = cost + markup

Remember Nathan, from page 16, with his idea for selling popcorn? He calculates that each box of popcorn will cost him 15¢ to make. The **price** he charges is the cost, plus an additional amount called the **markup**.

To decide how much markup to add, Nathan thinks about his potential customers and how much they might be happy to pay:

My customers will be my schoolmates. They don't have much money.

I'm broke.

Same here.

I've done some market research.

Market Research

Most people said that they would be willing to pay 40¢ for a box of popcorn.

What is the maximum you would pay for a box of popcorn?

Number of people who picked this option:

14
13
12
11
10

6
5
4
3
2
1

25¢ 30¢ 35¢ 40¢ 45¢ 50¢

Nathan also considers how much his competitors are charging for popcorn.

Next, Nathan thinks about how the price he sets might make customers *feel* about his product.

Setting the price at 39¢ means that Nathan has added a 24¢ markup to each box of popcorn. This means that for each box he sells, he gets to keep 24¢.

Selling to sellers

Sometimes a business sells a product directly to its **consumer** – the person who will actually use it. But businesses can often reach *more* consumers if they sell their product to *another business* instead. This other business could be a store, or a business that sells to stores.

Mike and his partner Mohan make and sell an electronic device called 'Kid Tracker', which enables parents to track the location of their child at a playground.

So Mike and Mohan decide to get Kid Trackers stocked in stores around the country. They take them to a **wholesaler**, a business selling to other businesses.

Next the wholesaler sells the product on to **retailers**, stores that sell products to consumers. The wholesaler adds a markup to the price when it sells it on.

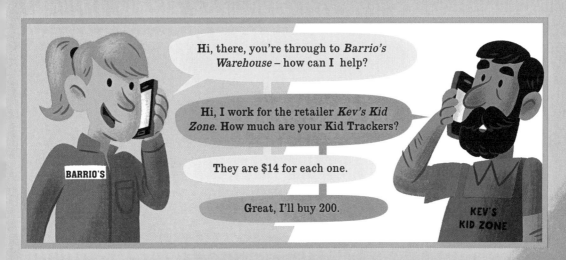

When the retailer sells the product on, it also adds a markup. *Kev's Kid Zone* sells the Kid Tracker for the same price that Mike and Mohan were originally charging.

Pricing tricks

You might think that price is just about making all the numbers add up. But pricing is part of marketing. It's a way to *persuade* someone to buy stuff. Here are some tricks that businesses often use.

Charge less, win customers

Some businesses set a very low price when they first launch a product. They don't make a profit at first, but they win over customers from competitors. This is called **penetration pricing**, which means it helps businesses enter – or penetrate – a market.

Look fancy, charge more

Some businesses set a very high price for their goods or services, to make people believe that they are superior. This is called **premium pricing**. Sometimes, more expensive things *are* of a higher grade. But not always...

Lose money here, make money there

Another approach is called **loss leader pricing**. A business charges a very low price on one product, in order to attract customers into the store. A customer ends up paying a high price for something else, so the business makes its profit that way.

Make one option look *too* pricey

Within a range of products, one option may have a very high price. This makes the cheaper ones seem like great value. This is called **decoy pricing**. The expensive choice is *only* there to push a customer to another product.

Give your business a personality

One way to attract customers is to create a personality for your business. This is known as a **brand.** The idea is that customers will then continue to buy from your business because they have an emotional connection to it, almost as if it were a friend.

Think about what kind of person you would like your business to be if it was a human being. Here are some characteristics to help you think it through:

approachable   TOUGH   influential   youthful   exciting

calm   successful   *thoughtful*   sophisticated   kind

friendly   *cozy*   fun   outdoorsy   serious   fun-loving

family-loving   athletic   competent   informal   sincere

Joe wants his café to have a *cozy* and *approachable* brand. He wants customers to get this impression every time they have contact with his business. For example:

The **name** of his business is informal

> Joe's place

The **font** means the style used to write text. Joe has picked a casual font.

A **logo** is a simple image to represent a business, or a distinctive way to write its name. For his, Joe has chosen an appealing hot drink.

The furniture, lighting and decoration is comfy and homely.

> Joe's place

Come on in, guys!

Pop in, pals!

Warm **colors** are used in the cafe.

Joe uses a friendly and welcoming **tone of voice** when talking or writing to customers.

Lila is talking about the brand for her new business with her friend Drew:

I am going to sell beautiful wooden bowls.

If my business was a person, it would be natural and also classy.

Nice! What will your business name be?

I'd like to call it *Lila Crafts* or *Lila Woodwork*.

Great! Maybe your logo could have the shade and texture of wood in it. Should I help you design it?

Yes, please. Let's decide on the web address, too!

Later...

They both feel natural, but the top one feels more classy.

www.lilacrafts.com

This could be the web address.

Oh dear! It looks like Lilac Rafts, as if you're making purple boats, not wooden bowls.

Oh yes you're right! It'll have to be Lila Woodwork instead!

Watch out for these kinds of pitfalls. Test your brand to make sure the message that it conveys feels consistent across all the ways you will communicate it.

Find words that sell

Successful businesses find a powerful way to describe their product to explain why it is worth buying. These persuasive words are called **marketing messages** and often appeal to people's emotions.

Remember Martha, from page 18? She's launching a business selling T-shirts. Her friend Elise is helping her write her marketing messages.

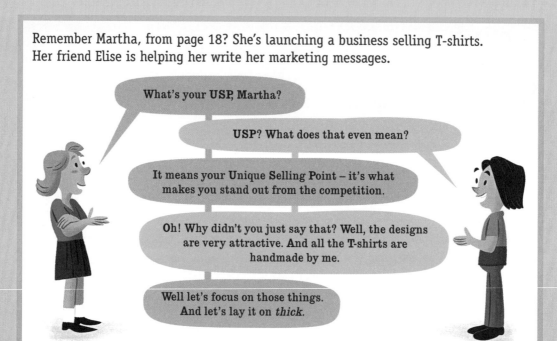

What's your USP, Martha?

USP? What does that even mean?

It means your Unique Selling Point – it's what makes you stand out from the competition.

Oh! Why didn't you just say that? Well, the designs are very attractive. And all the T-shirts are handmade by me.

Well let's focus on those things. And let's lay it on *thick*.

Elise suggests some marketing messages and explains why she's written them.

You're beautiful. You belong in a <u>beautiful</u> T-shirt.

Telling people they are beautiful is flattery, which means making them feel good about themselves.

Martha's T-shirts

"Individually crafted" sounds exclusive. Having something that not many others have makes people feel special.

T-shirts individually crafted by a <u>local fashion whiz</u>.

"Local fashion whiz" is a catchy way to describe yourself. People remember catchy phrases.

Businesses hope to trigger emotions that will prompt potential customers to buy their product. This might be a negative emotion, such as fear, or a positive emotion, such as feeling appreciated.

Words can only do so much...

It's hard to sell something useless, however much you work on the words. That's why businesses spend lots of time developing their product so that it matches what customers want (see page 16 about market research).

It's also against the law to lie about goods or services. So in order to make your stuff *sound great*, make sure it *really is great*!

Spread the word

Marketing messages are no use unless potential customers hear or read them. So businesses spread the word in lots of different ways. This is called **promotion**.

Here, Martha and Elise are promoting *Martha's T-shirts* all over their home town of Doxford.

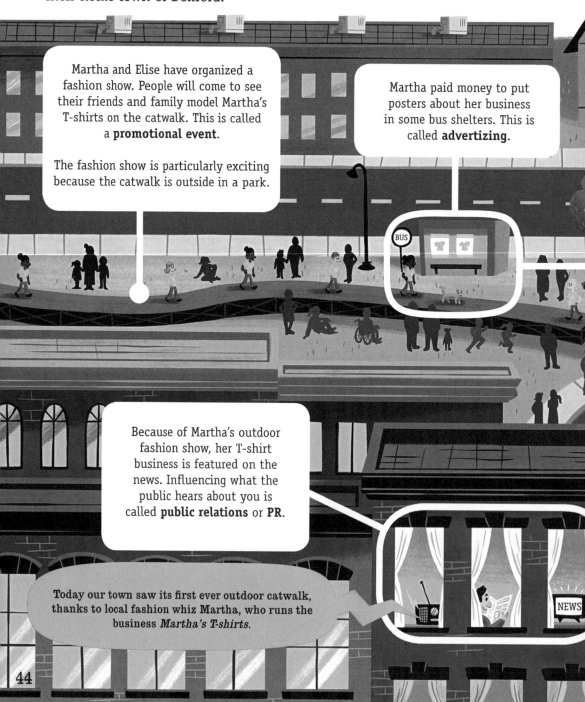

Martha and Elise have organized a fashion show. People will come to see their friends and family model Martha's T-shirts on the catwalk. This is called a **promotional event**.

The fashion show is particularly exciting because the catwalk is outside in a park.

Martha paid money to put posters about her business in some bus shelters. This is called **advertizing**.

Because of Martha's outdoor fashion show, her T-shirt business is featured on the news. Influencing what the public hears about you is called **public relations** or **PR**.

Today our town saw its first ever outdoor catwalk, thanks to local fashion whiz Martha, who runs the business *Martha's T-shirts*.

This person has received a letter through his front door about Martha's T-shirts. This is called **direct marketing**.

Unexpectedly, a cat strolls down the catwalk. Someone posts a video of it online, which gets shared 5,000 times. This makes Martha happy because her poster is visible in the video. A video that spreads quickly online is sometimes called **viral**.

Martha has paid for **online ads**, which only appear when someone types 'T-shirt' and the name of the town into a search engine.

Martha and Elise are handing out coupons giving people money off, called a **discount**, to encourage sales.

MARTHA'S T-SHIRTS
10% off
Discount coupon

People talking casually to each other about the attraction of a product is called **word of mouth** promotion.

I've just been to a fashion show in **Doxford** and the T-shirts are awesome. Look up *Martha's T-shirts* – I think you'll love them.

Tailored messages

Often, businesses don't send the same marketing messages to everyone. Instead, they find out as much as they can about their customers and then target them personally. To do this, businesses first gather huge amounts of information. This is called **data**.

This is Annie. In the last week, she shopped at a supermarket, used a guitar tuning app, logged on to social media and wore her fitness tracker every day.

This is what businesses know about Annie:

Annie is between the ages of 18 and 25.

She eats lots of granola, eggs and chocolate cookies.

Annie played her guitar last night and spends a lot of time in Ashville.

ASHVILLE

She is interested in snowboarding and lives in Apricot Creek.

Annie ran eight miles yesterday, and six miles last week.

How can businesses know things about Annie?

Supermart knows Annie's age because last week she filled in a survey they sent her.

Supermart knows what Annie eats, because she has a loyalty card that she scans each time she shops there.

Guitar Heaven knows where and when Annie plays her guitar because she uses their tuning app, and she's enabled location services in the app.

On social media, Annie has liked a page about snowboarding, and has Apricot Creek set as the place she lives.

Active! knows about Annie's runs, as she wears one of their fitness trackers, linked to an app on her phone.

What can they do to take advantage of the information they have?

Supermart sends Annie discount vouchers for products she often buys. They also send her vouchers for cereal bars. She hasn't bought one yet...

...but other granola-eaters age 18-25 do, according to Supermart's loyalty card data.

Guitar Heaven sends Annie an email about an upcoming Guitar Show in Ashville.

Snow Mountain Ski Resort – near Apricot Creek – targets Annie with ads through social media. They run ads for day tickets whenever the snowboarding conditions are good.

Active! sends Annie motivating tips to her phone. She finds the tips helpful, so feels loyal to *Active!* and might buy more stuff from the business in the future.

Marketing disasters

Some businesses promote their products in ways that are dishonest, unfair or irresponsible. Whether or not a business actually breaks the law, its reputation is severely damaged if it uses unethical marketing tactics. Here are some businesses that got caught.

False promises

A US-based business called *Tarr Inc.* promoted wrinkle creams on the internet using false claims.

It is against the law to mislead people in marketing, and *Tarr Inc.* was ordered to pay $6 million in fines.

REAL EXAMPLE

INSTANT WRINKLE REDUCER

LOOK 10 YEARS **YOUNGER** IN LESS THAN **4 WEEKS!**

I'll never fit into my summer clothes.

Take new XLS Medical Max Strength

REAL EXAMPLE

Dangerous messages

In Ireland, healthcare company *Omega Pharma* was ordered to remove a TV advertisement for diet pills.

The ad showed a woman complaining about her weight, when she was a normal, healthy size. It could encourage people to lose weight when they don't need to.

Unwanted marketing

A Canadian business called *CompuFinder*, which sold training courses, sent hundreds of people emails without asking their permission. This is often called **spam**.

Under Canada's law against spam, *CompuFinder* was fined $200,000.

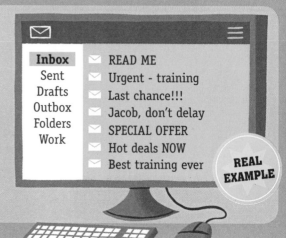

Inbox
Sent
Drafts
Outbox
Folders
Work

READ ME
Urgent - training
Last chance!!!
Jacob, don't delay
SPECIAL OFFER
Hot deals NOW
Best training ever

REAL EXAMPLE

Targeting children

A young Swedish vlogger broke advertising rules, when she enthused about a range of dolls in an online video. She failed to say that she was advertising them for the dolls' manufacturer, *GR-Trading AS*.

Children can't always spot when a company is trying to sell to them, so marketing must be *clearly labeled* as marketing.

x 2,300   31 comments

False price comparisons

CATALOG

An Australian business named *Zamel's* promoted necklaces and bracelets with a big discount.

Customers thought they were getting a good deal, but in fact the products had never been on sale at the higher price. This is against the law and *Zamel's* was ordered to pay a penalty of $250,000.

Was $275
Now $149!!

Offensive content

MIRACLE MATTRESS

CLOSED

CLOSED
CLOSED
CLOSED

Miracle Mattress was an American business selling mattresses. But in 2016, it made a promotional video with a jokey reference to the 2001 terrorist attack on New York, in which nearly 3,000 people died.

There was a furious reaction to the video, with thousands of people complaining. The reputational damage was so serious that the owner had to close the business.

Wherever you are, you should think about how different groups of people might feel about your marketing. If you're not sure, do some market research.

Chapter 3:
Keeping track of money

It might not sound very exciting, but keeping a record of the money coming in and going out of a business is essential for it to succeed. These records are known as **accounts**. They show how much money the business is making and how many taxes it should pay to the government.

About a third of businesses fail in the first two years, mostly because they've run out of money. By keeping a close eye on their accounts, businesses can plan ahead, avoid unpleasant surprises and have a better chance of success.

In and out

Money coming *into* a business from selling products is known as **revenue**. The amounts going *out* and being spent on things the business needs to operate are known as **costs**.

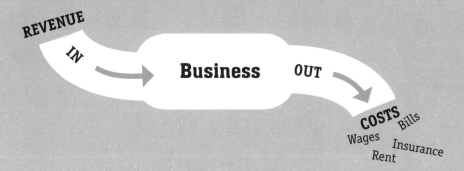

Meena has set up a monthly magazine, which she sells at school. Here are the costs involved in making the October edition and the revenue she gets from selling it.

So the total cost for making 100 magazines is: **$20 + $15 + $2 = $37**

Revenue

"We sold 90 magazines for $1 each. So my revenue is $90."

"I'm so happy people like my magazine! It sold so well that I've made more revenue than I spent on costs."

Quantity of magazines → 90 x $1 = $90 ←
Price — Revenue

Keeping records

The simplest way of keeping track of costs and revenue is to write them down in a record book as you go along.

MAY
OUT:
May 25th
  print & staple: $15
May 31st
  wages: $20
May 31st
  cookies: $2

Total cost: $37

IN:
May 26th
  sales: $30
May 27th
  sales: $40
May 28th
  sales: $20

Total revenue: $90

Printease
42-44 Ink Road
- - - - - - - - - -
Chk 4001   May 25 11:38
- - - - - - - - - -
100 copies: $15

- - - - - - - - - -
Subtotal $15
Payment $15

A date and short description will help jog your memory when you come back to that page.

Keep bills and receipts to help you remember exactly what you spent and earned.

Keeping records might seem boring, but it's the only way to know how much money you're making. What's more, you have to make a note of this by law in order to pay the right amount of taxes (see more on page 58). Many entrepreneurs hire a person known as an **accountant** to help with their accounts.

Making money

When a business makes more money than it spends, it makes a profit. It's one of the main goals of any business.

Profit = revenue – costs.

NOVEMBER: Meena's magazine has been selling well at school.

> I've made $90 of revenue this month and spent $37.

> So you've made a profit of $90-$37=$53.

Meena can use the profit to...

Reward herself for all her hard work.

Invest – spend it on improving and growing the business.

Save in case the business doesn't do so well in the future.

> Woop! I could spend some of my profit on the new book I wanted.

RESCUE MISSION

> I could start paying my friend to illustrate the covers. The magazine will look even better so more people will want to buy it.

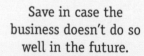

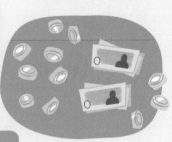

Losing money

Sometimes, businesses don't make enough money from selling their products to cover their costs, so they *lose* money. This might be because they're not selling enough, their prices are too low, their costs are too high or not enough people actually want their product.

DECEMBER: Meena's magazine hasn't been selling well. Lots of her friends need to save their money to buy Christmas presents.

This month, we only sold 20 copies of the magazine.

So my costs are higher than my revenue: I've spent $37 and only made $20. I've lost $17 from trading.

Meena can reduce her losses by...

Changing the way she does business.

Next year, I could get local businesses to pay for advertisements in the December edition. That way I could give the magazine away for free.

the ZINE

FREE edition

Cutting costs

Or I could sell a smaller version of the magazine which will only cost $15 to make.

the ZINE

Issue 3

the ZINE

Pocket

Increasing revenue

Or I could start selling the magazine at the youth club, to try to get more customers for each issue.

Planning ahead

A business has to make enough money to pay its bills, suppliers and workers and these costs often need to get paid before any revenue comes in. Businesses have to keep an eye on **cash flow** – the movement of money in and out of their bank account.

Meet the co-owners of *SunCatcher*, an energy company based in Europe, where people use a type of money called Euros (€). They're planning to build their next solar farm for some new clients.

By the end of October the business will have run out of cash and we won't be able to pay our November bills.

We'll finish the project in December. So by the time the customer gets around to paying us, it'll be the new year.

€600,000 payment

OCTOBER   **NOVEMBER**   **DECEMBER**   **JANUARY**

€100,000 monthly costs

Where's our money?!

So the business needs to plan ahead to avoid running out of money before January. One or more of these ideas might solve the cash flow problem.

We could ask to be paid in chunks every month rather than all at once at the end.

Or agree with suppliers to delay paying them.

Or get a loan from the bank until we get paid.

Or take on a smaller project on the side that would bring in regular small amounts of money.

Or sell something we own, such as equipment or a building.

Paying taxes

A business can't simply keep all the money it makes. It has to give some of it back to society, by paying taxes. **Tax** is money a government collects from people, both as individuals and businesses, to pay for **public services** such as roads and schools.

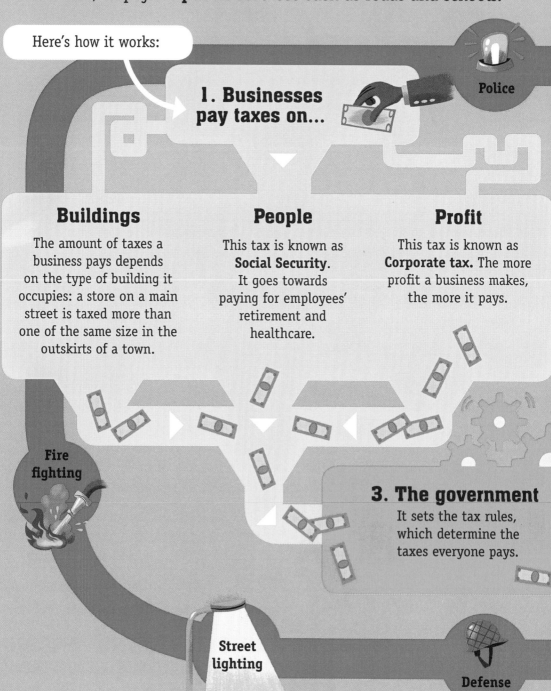

Here's how it works:

1. Businesses pay taxes on...

Police

Buildings

The amount of taxes a business pays depends on the type of building it occupies: a store on a main street is taxed more than one of the same size in the outskirts of a town.

People

This tax is known as **Social Security**. It goes towards paying for employees' retirement and healthcare.

Profit

This tax is known as **Corporate tax.** The more profit a business makes, the more it pays.

Fire fighting

3. The government

It sets the tax rules, which determine the taxes everyone pays.

Street lighting

Defense

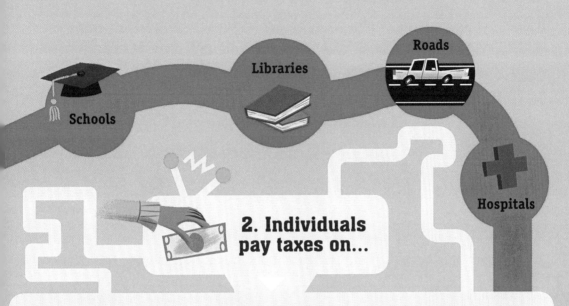

Schools

Libraries

Roads

Hospitals

2. Individuals pay taxes on...

Things you buy

The price of most things includes a tax known as **Sales Tax**.

Money you earn

These taxes are known as **Income Tax** and **Social Security** contributions.

Your possessions

In most countries, individuals pay taxes on property, or shares they own and anything they inherit.

The government uses taxes to fund public services. Most people agree that taxes help a society work well.

Justice system

Waste disposal

4. Public services

These kinds of services benefit everyone. Here are some examples...

Keeping honest accounts

By law, every business has to keep accounts which give an honest summary of its activities. This is important, not only for the business itself, but for investors and the government too.

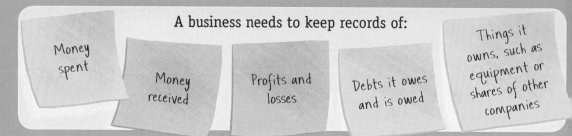

A business needs to keep records of:

Money spent

Money received

Profits and losses

Debts it owes and is owed

Things it owns, such as equipment or shares of other companies

Accountants help businesses do their accounts, but it's not always straightforward.

The bigger a company gets, the harder it is to keep track of it all.

Managers might want us to exaggerate how well their company is doing, to make them look better to potential investors.

Or they might even want to make things look *worse*, so they can pay fewer taxes.

And if a business's accounts aren't honest...

The business can't make sensible decisions as it is basing them on false information.

The government might not receive the right amount of taxes.

Investors will be risking their money without knowing how well the business is doing.

I wouldn't have bought that machine, if the manager hadn't exaggerated how much money we made last year...

The money the government loses in tax revenue is money that won't go to schools and hospitals.

Oh no! We *thought* it was a successful company. Now it's failed and we've lost lots of money!

So it makes moral sense *and* business sense to keep honest accounts.

Is trying to pay fewer taxes OK?

Businesses often try to pay fewer taxes to save money. Some rules are deliberately designed by the government to help certain businesses pay less, for example lower taxes for startups. But sometimes, big businesses escape taxes by finding **loopholes**, or ways around tax rules. Some people argue this is cheating the system – even if it's legal. What do you think?

Speek Mobile does most of its business in India, but it is registered in the Cayman Islands, where the government collects fewer taxes. This arrangement is perfectly legal, but it means the Indian government loses out on millions in tax revenue.

I run *Speek Mobile*.

I'm a *Speek Mobile* customer.

I know it looks bad, but I think paying fewer taxes is actually **OK**.

Looks *bad*? It looks terrible! I have to pay taxes, why shouldn't you?

Think about it, all that money we save on taxes is money we can spend on making better, cheaper products for *you*. I'm not spending it on fancy clothes for me.

Yes, but the money you save could have gone to the government, who might have fixed the road by my house.

But if we did pay taxes in India, the price of our products would go up. And then you and your family probably wouldn't be able to afford a phone. Our product shouldn't only be for the super-rich.

Well don't worry, I won't be your customer any longer anyway. I'd rather give my money to a company that behaves fairly.

Wouldn't I? But there isn't a cheaper phone on the market...

Why businesses fail

The biggest risk of running a business is it might run out of money and fail. Lots do, especially in the first couple of years. Even very successful business people, such as the American inventor and entrepreneur Thomas Edison, experienced failure...

REAL EXAMPLE

From the lightbulb to the telephone transmitter, my inventions and businesses changed the world.

But let me tell you, it's not been an easy ride...

Poor market research

In 1869, I was 22 and I'd just registered my first invention. It was a machine that counted votes and would save lots of time during elections.

Here's my amazing invention: the Automatic Vote Counter. You'll love it!

Young man look here, we don't *want* machines to count votes.

Humans are much more... reliable.

I never want to build something that nobody wants to buy again.

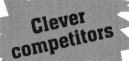

In 1875, I launched a battery-powered pen that helped make copies of documents. People loved it, but not for long.

THE COPYING PEN

Special copying ink

That was quick. They've taken my idea and improved it. No one will want my pen any more.

Just like Edison's pen but with no messy batteries.

Then in 1881, my talking doll, which should have sold well, had to be taken off the market after only a few weeks.

It's voice is just so annoying!

Good idea, badly executed

In 1904, I started a new business that sold my inventions in Germany. When the country found itself at war, people stopped coming to the store, and it had to shut.

Edison's store, Germany

Global events

Lots of entrepreneurs have had failed businesses or ideas. They learn from the failure, start again and launch a better business. In some cases, failure can even become an opportunity.

I once tried and failed to build an undersea telegraph. But a technique I discovered helped me to improve the telephone – which sold really well!

63

The end of the road

If a business runs out of money and can't repay its debts, it has failed. But the story doesn't just end there. Here's what can happen...

BREAKING NEWS

Transaero, a Russian airline, has run out of money due to falling sales. It can't repay $4 billion of debt.

November 2015

REAL EXAMPLE

HELP!

First, *Transaero* owners tried to make a deal with **creditors**, the people they owed money to. *Transaero* asked for more time to pay its debts.

The creditors said no.

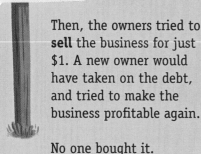

FOR SALE

Then, the owners tried to **sell** the business for just $1. A new owner would have taken on the debt, and tried to make the business profitable again.

No one bought it.

CLOSED

Eventually, the airline had to shut down and sell what it owned, in order to pay off as much of the debt as it could. This is known as **liquidation.** (It's called **bankruptcy** for a sole proprietor.)

This is the life!

It's not always bad

Lots of businesses close without any debts. As long as owners can pay their last bills and taxes, all they have to do is fill in some paperwork and then they're free to move on.

Who loses out?

When *Transaero* had to close, lots of people lost money and even their livelihoods. It took a very long time to sort through the company's finances, and most people were never repaid in full.

Suppliers

My company's not been paid for lots of fuel.

We were building 38 planes for *Transaero*. They'll never pay for them now.

Employees

Thousands of us lost our jobs.

All the money each of us invested in the company is now lost.

Customers

We'd booked our vacation but now we can't go.

Shareholders

Creditors

We loaned the airline lots of money, which we'll never get back in full.

Lots of people may depend on a business, so businesses have a responsibility not to take unnecessary risks.

Chapter 4:
People in business

Businesses need **people**. Inspiring **leaders** and teams of motivated **employees** can transform a business. A business benefits from a diverse range of skills and experience, which many **managers** keep in mind when they are hiring.

A business is constantly affected by **customers'** decisions about what to buy. And it's the responsibility of a business to protect **consumers** who use its products, as well as the **community** in the local area.

Who's who in business?

It takes many people to run a big business. Here are the different roles involved in a large business that makes electric bikes.

The **Chief Executive Officer** (CEO), sometimes called a **Managing Director** (MD), is in charge of managing the whole business.

A **Board of Directors** makes long-term decisions about the business. For example, they hire and fire the CEO.

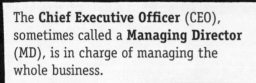

> Since I took over, our sales of electric bikes are up.

> But why aren't they up as much as you promised?

> Let me explain...

The **staff** is split into different teams, each working in a different area of the business.

> We work in marketing.

> I'm in charge of the business's accounts.

Shareholders own a portion of the business, known as shares. The value of their shares increases when the business does well, and decreases when it doesn't. If they sell their shares when the business is doing well, they will make money.

SHARE PRICES

> I should have sold my shares last week – they were worth more then.

Shareholders elect the Board of Directors at an annual meeting.

EAZY ELECTRIC CYCLES

Managers run a particular team or department.

> Hey Production Team! We've got a busy day ahead: six orders to complete by 5pm!

> I manage the sales team.

> I build bikes.

> OK boss!

> I test them for quality.

Managers and staff are **employees**: they work for the business in return for wages.

The CEO and Directors are also paid by the business, but the rules about how this works differ in different countries.

People outside the business – its **customers** and the **community** living nearby – are affected by how well the business is run. See pages 78-81.

> I bought this electric bike yesterday. Now I'm off to tell all my friends.

How do you lead?

There's a lot to think about if you're in charge. Luana runs a cruise ship business called *Topaz Sailing*. She does all of these things in her role as CEO.

Creates a vision for the future

Luana has a clear, ambitious idea for what the business should be like in five or ten years time.

In ten years, *Topaz Sailing* will be the most famous and successful cruise business in the world.

It will take millions of new customers from China on cruises around Asia and the Pacific.

Inspires people

Luana communicates her vision to her staff and motivates them to make it a reality.

We will be the biggest and the best.

And it will be because of the work **YOU** do.

TOPAZ SAILING

Hurrah

Yes!

YEAH

Innovates

She has a flow of creative, exciting ideas that make the business stand out.

Rather than huge, impersonal cruise ships, we will build smaller, friendlier ships.

1970s themed cruise

Jazz Cruise

We'll offer different themed ships, so passengers can choose entertainment they will love.

Management

Luana organizes projects and staff in a sensible way so the business runs smoothly. She assigns money to different projects, in a plan called a **budget**.

> I must check if we're going over budget for building the new ships.

> I must bring in some new staff – we need 23 more people in Guangzhou by the end of 2019.

(In some very large businesses, CEOs delegate management to other people, to keep their own minds free for creative and long-term thinking.)

Develops employees

Luana helps staff to gain new skills so they can excel at their jobs.

> I'd like you to make a speech at our shareholders' meeting this month.

> When I retire, she could become **CEO** – so I want her to gain confidence.

Makes difficult decisions

To keep the business on track, Luana sometimes has to make herself unpopular.

> We're cutting the cruise to the Bering Strait. We're not making enough money on it. Sadly, you will lose your job.

Leading a micro-business

Leaders of micro-businesses (businesses which employ fewer than 10 people) need to do *all* of the things above. But they may *also* need to do the day-to-day work themselves, from finances, to marketing, to actually making the product.

Diversity

Employing people from different backgrounds is known as **diversity.** Teams can be diverse from the point of view of age, ethnicity, religion, gender, sexuality, disability or level of education. It makes sense for a workforce to include people from **minority groups**, which are groups that can face discrimination. Find out why below.

I think it's wrong that there aren't more people of ethnic minority backgrounds on our team.

I just hire the most competent people. Their ethnicity isn't important.

But we want to sell our products to people of all backgrounds. How can we give customers what they want if we don't understand them?

You're from an ethnic minority, can't you tell us?

That's not how it works! I can't speak on behalf of *everyone* who isn't white. What we need is a team of people with diverse perspectives, lifestyles and experiences.

But why would that help when the team's full of clever people already?

Listen – when the business is going well, you don't notice that the team has a similar way of thinking. But when we hit a challenge, we need a broader range of creative ideas.

OK. But why aren't more people from ethnic minority backgrounds applying for jobs?

We're looking in the wrong places when we hire! There are so many talented people out there who would do excellent work here.

You really think so?

Yes! And I think it's only fair to give everyone the opportunity to work here.

I'm convinced! Let's do everything we can to increase diversity in our business.

Hiring

When businesses give someone new a job – known as **hiring** – they have to make sure that person is right for the role, and that the process is fair. These are the kinds of steps they go through.

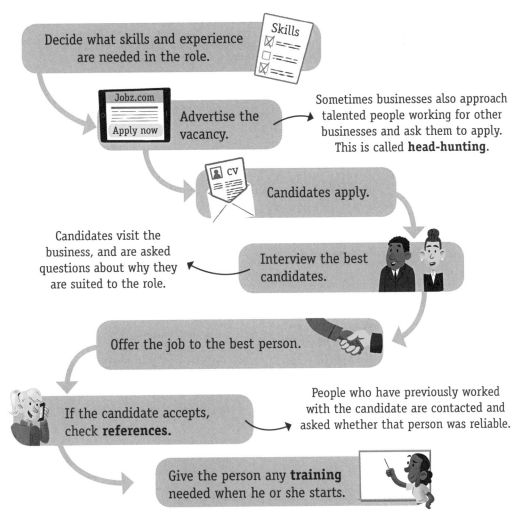

Decide what skills and experience are needed in the role.

Skills

Advertise the vacancy.

Jobz.com
Apply now

Sometimes businesses also approach talented people working for other businesses and ask them to apply. This is called **head-hunting**.

Candidates apply.

CV

Candidates visit the business, and are asked questions about why they are suited to the role.

Interview the best candidates.

Offer the job to the best person.

If the candidate accepts, check **references.**

People who have previously worked with the candidate are contacted and asked whether that person was reliable.

Give the person any **training** needed when he or she starts.

To get the best candidates and hire in a fair way, businesses can do the following:

Advertise jobs on websites and in newspapers which have minority groups as their audience.

Get someone in the business to take people's names and ages off job applications. This stops the person hiring from making assumptions about someone's ability based on their name and age.

Offer paid work placements to help poorer young people get their first step into the business.

Teamwork

Businesses are often structured into teams of employees, who either work in similar roles or on the same project. Working together, people in a team can often achieve more than if they were just getting on with their jobs on their own.

Teams often have a mix of people with different skills and weaknesses.

I've found us a new client!

Well done, you're so good at that! Have you logged them in our database?

Um, no. I always forget how to.

I'll do it! I like getting everything in order.

People improve their ideas by bouncing them around in a team.

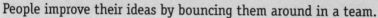

I've thought of a name for our new beauty cream: "Face Shine."

Hmm. No. People don't want shiny faces.

OK. Do I mean "glow" not "shine?"

Surely, yes.

How about "Natural Glow?"

Much better.

People in a team can support each other.

I'm sorry, I'm sick today. I can't deliver the bread.

Don't worry! The team will cover your rounds. Get well soon!

I really appreciate it. Thank you.

Motivating people

Employees who like their jobs and are committed to the business are usually much more productive. So it's in the interest of managers to keep them happy. Here's one way to approach it.

Step 1: fix bad working conditions

Poor pay

 An annoying manager

Fear of losing a job

 Difficult relationships with teammates

Frustrating paperwork

When these conditions are wrong, it demotivates people. But however much you eliminate these kinds of problems, it still won't make people *happy*. It'll just stop them from being *unhappy*.

Step 2: give workers job satisfaction

For workers to be happy, motivated and productive, they need the following:

Some control over their work

Opportunities to progress

Responsibility

A feeling of purpose

A sense of achievement

Recognition for their hard work

A chance to develop new skills

A range of tasks that matches their interests

Good managers aim to achieve as many of these as possible for their staff.

Workers' rights

Business leaders have more power than their employees. This can make employees vulnerable – they can be driven too hard, paid too little or put in danger. To protect them, there are international rules about how to treat workers, known as **workers' rights**.

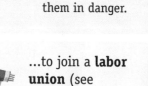

Everyone has the right...

...to choose whether to work.

People mustn't be forced to work or punished if they don't work.

...to a childhood.

Children mustn't work if it disrupts their education or puts them in danger.

...to fair pay.

...to be free from discrimination.

For example, a woman or someone from an ethnic minority mustn't be given fewer opportunities than another worker.

...to be safe and healthy at work.

...to join a **labor union** (see opposite page).

...to paid time off every year, known as **paid vacation**.

In reality, workers get different rights around the world, depending on the laws in a particular country.

I live in the **USA**. There's no law here about paid vacation, so it's up to my employer to decide. Sadly, I only get 5 days a year.

Oh what a shame! I live in the **UK**. The law here gives me 28 days of paid vacation each year.

Lucky you! And after my baby was born, I only got unpaid maternity leave.

I live in Sweden. My partner and I shared 480 days of paid parental leave after we had our baby.

People power

Often workers want better conditions, such as increased pay, more paid vacation time, or a safer work environment. They have more power if they join together to make their demands to their employer. If the employer refuses, they may go on **strike**...

Organizations called **labor unions** represent the interests of workers with similar jobs. Labor unions support workers to make their collective demands to their employer, and can help to organize strikes.

In most places, it's illegal for employers to stop workers from joining a labor union. As well as being a legal obligation, it also builds positive relationships within a business if leaders respect union activities.

Consumers and customers

The people *using* the products or services of a business are called **consumers**. They are not always the same as **customers**, who *buy* them. Businesses have very important relationships with both.

Consumers have power. If a baby hates one kind of baby food, the baby's parent won't buy it again. The parent may also influence other customers, for example by writing an online review. This, in turn, will impact on the business's plans.

The best companies don't wait for feedback from consumers. They involve the people who will be buying and using the product as they design it. See page 16, about market research.

Protecting consumers

The law protects consumers from dishonest and careless businesses. There are some things it's illegal to do in most countries.

 Sell unsafe products

Sell products that are fakes, such as a fake designer handbag

Deliver services to a poor standard

Advertise dishonestly (see pages 48-49)

In many places, customers have a legal right to return a product and get their money back if it is faulty. This is called a **refund**.

Product recall

If a business realizes it is selling something unsafe, it may ask everyone who bought it to bring it back. This is called **product recall**.

Instead of waiting for an accident to happen, the business can limit the damage to its reputation, and reduce the risk that it will be taken to court by an angry consumer.

Product recall notice

REAL EXAMPLE

Some *Sony* batteries inside *Dell*™ notebook computers are at risk of catching fire. If you bought a *Dell* notebook between April 2004 and July 2006, check the battery model and serial number. Affected batteries will be replaced.

Complaining

JUST STOP IT!

NO!

Consumers can – and do – complain to businesses when they are disappointed.

But if a business has broken the *law*, consumers can object to the *government*. If many people have been affected, organizations supporting consumers may bring them together to make a joint complaint.

These organizations also give consumers information about their rights, and produce independent reviews of goods and services.

Community impacts

A business impacts the people living around it: the local **community**. This can be positive, bringing money, jobs and services to an area.

The local community benefits from *Blenheim Street Theater* in multiple ways.

Creating jobs and bringing in new customers to an area are positive impacts that can have a ripple effect:

1. A local business creates jobs.
2. Employees have more money to spend.
3. More money is spent in *other* local businesses.
4. Many local businesses thrive and expand.
1. A local business attracts customers to *other* local businesses.
2. Many local businesses thrive and expand.

But a business can also have a negative impact on a local community.

A business's working hours can affect family life.

Grandma! Where are Mommy and Daddy?

They're at work in the factory again, dear.

Will I see them before bed?

No, they only get back very late these days since the boss made them work longer hours.

Accidents can cause pollution.

This oil spill has ruined everything! The oil is all over our land and in our water.

How are we going to fish and grow food now?

Absolute Oil

A business can cause bad traffic.

The roads are gridlocked these days. AAAARGH!

I blame that new supermarket that just opened.

MEGASUPER

Sometimes whole communities need to move to make room for a business's operations.

I miss our town. It's so sad that it is now completely covered with water.

I wish they'd never built this hydroelectric dam.

POWERDAM

It's unethical for business leaders to ignore negative impacts on the local community. It's also shortsighted; a business can be taken to court and forced to pay vast amounts of money to a community for damage it has caused.

Some harmful businesses never even get off the ground. Businesses often need permission from either local or national government to operate, especially for major activities such as drilling for oil. A community can protest against plans, making it less likely for a destructive business to be given permission.

Chapter 5:
Making a product

To turn an idea into a **product**, lots of things need to happen. Businesses have to source materials – often from different places around the world. They then need the right people, tools and machines to make the product. Finally, the product has to make its way to somewhere a customer will buy it.

The challenge is to do all that quickly and cheaply, while still creating a product that customers love, and that doesn't cause harm either to people or the environment.

How stuff gets made

The process of creating goods and services is known as **production**. There are lots of ways of making any one thing. So entrepreneurs need to pick the method best suited to their product.

One of a kind

When products are made one by one, it's known as **job production**. It works best for unique, one-off products, where each customer has specific needs.

In batches

Another way to make a product is in groups, or **batches**. It's generally quicker and cheaper than making things individually.

One size fits all

When businesses produce huge quantities of identical goods in a factory with specialized machinery, it's called **mass production**. It's expensive to set up, but once you're up and running, it's a quick and cheap way of making things.

We make a million cakes in this factory every day. We do this by splitting the work into tasks.

The conveyor belt moves the cakes around the factory for us, which saves lots of time.

My task is to make sure each cake is the right size and shape when it comes out the oven.

Once the system is set up, it's not easy to change the product...

...you can have a cake in any shape as long as it's round!

I test the cake mix.

I want the cheapest cake I can get.

Mass customization

This is a way of producing goods combines mass production with some element of customization.

BakeMaster.com

Add a personalized message for free!

Happy Birthday Alex!

I'm happy with a standard cake, but it's even better with a personalized message.

85

How does stuff *really* get made?

Production of day-to-day things often involves complicated, worldwide networks of businesses. This is known as a **supply chain**, and it can make it unclear who is ultimately responsible for making the product, how it gets made and with what materials.

For example, here's how a supply chain works for this pair of shoes:

1 The shoes are designed in the USA.

2 The thread is spun in Bulgaria.

3 The insole is produced in China.

4 The synthetic leather is made in Japan.

The leather is made from American polyurethane.

5 The lining, label, shoelace and fabric are made in Taiwan.

The cotton comes from India and the polyester from Saudi Arabia.

6 The rubber outsoles are cast in Indonesia.

The rubber is sourced from a factory in Thailand.

7 The parts are made into the finished shoe in China.

8 The shoes are shipped to shops around the world.

Each supplier has its own supplier, and so on...

Here are some reasons why businesses have global supply chains.

Good, low-cost materials

Countries often specialize and become world leaders in making something well and inexpensively.

The cheapest workforce

Businesses can take advantage of lower salaries in some parts of the world.

Don't know, don't care

Global supply chains can bring jobs and money to poorer parts of the world. But they also make it easy for bad working conditions to go unnoticed and unchallenged by big brands and customers.

For example, here are some workers in a factory in Bangladesh:

Every hour I stitch the seams and pockets on 120 pairs of jeans. I do that 10 hours a day, 6 days a week, 300 days a year.

We're only paid $80 per month, but that's still better than what I was earning before.

If you're buying a pair of jeans for $25, what do you expect our working conditions to be?

Vulnerable workers making cheap products for the rest of the world need to be protected. Businesses can help by making sure they know how their products are being made and by whom, and insisting on high standards. Communicating that information then helps consumers buy responsibly.

I always used to buy the cheapest jeans, but now I look out for ethical clothes.

Making more with less

If a business can make things **more efficiently** – *better*, *faster* or more *cheaply* than its rivals – it will attract more customers. So businesses are constantly finding ways to improve their production

Lean production

In the 1970s, engineers at *Toyota*, a Japanese carmaker, developed something called **lean production**. This aims to cut costs by reducing different types of waste. Here's what Toyota engineer, Shigeo Shingo, recommended.

REAL EXAMPLE

Don't...

...waste time

Employees can waste time moving between buildings, looking for tools or materials. Any delays in the process can lead to much bigger delays later on.

So, for example, keeping tools at hand height saves time reaching for them.

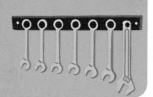

...complicate things

Unless a feature is really important to the consumer, it's not worth adding it. It will create costs without adding extra value.

Who needs a heated steering wheel anyway?

...overstock

For production to run smoothly, businesses need to have supplies, or **stock**, of materials ready. However, stock costs money to store and maintain.

To minimize the amount of stock, it could be ordered to arrive as it's needed and taken straight to the factory floor.

...overproduce

If businesses make things they don't sell, it's a waste of resources and money.

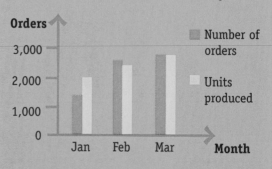

For example, in January this firm overproduced by 500 units. To avoid this, they could wait for customers to place an order before starting production.

Keep improving

If a business stops improving, it's almost inevitable that someone else will come along with a better product or process and win over customers. Providing more training for employees is one way of improving production. Here are some more.

Investing in machinery

We used to spray paint cars by hand, now machines do it instead.

It's faster and saves money, but the people who used to do it lost their jobs.

Pooling ideas

Every week, we ask everyone in the factory to come up with ideas for how to improve the way we work.

We believe solutions to problems are more likely to come from people on the factory floor than from someone sitting at a desk far away.

This system was developed at *Toyota* and is known as **kaizen**, which means "change for the better" in Japanese.

Learning from the best

Comparing your business to others is known as **benchmarking**.

Thanks for showing us around your factory!

We try to learn from how other big factories do things.

Quality sells

A **quality** product is one that meets a customer's expectations. If customers love a product, they're more likely to buy it again and recommend it to others. Entrepreneurs value quality, as it helps a product sell itself.

Quality at every step

This internet browser has won lots of loyal customers. Here's why.

 SATURN   It's the only browser out there!

OVERVIEW	REVIEWS	SUPPORT	RELATED

Easy to access

"Downloading the browser is really straightforward. The instructions are in a big, clear font, and there's an audio version too. I'd recommend it to other internet newbies out there."

Miguel, Canada

Customizable

"It's amazing! You can set the browser up exactly as you want it. If you want a map of the stars and the latest volleyball news on your homepage, you can have it."

Yi Wei, Singapore

Simple to get rid of

"This browser wasn't for me, but at least it was easy to uninstall!"

Iku, Japan

Thoroughly tested

"An early version of the browser was released for experienced computer coders. So I was one of the first to test it and point out problems. I loved being involved in the process."

Nina, Germany

Helpful team

"I couldn't work out how to customize the toolbar. I messaged the help team and they got back to me really quickly. They've been trained to be friendly **AND** helpful. Thumbs up."

Adaeze, Nigeria

They listen

"I wrote in to complain about download times. Thanks for apologizing and fixing the problem!"

Oliver, Ireland

How much quality?

Quality products cost more to produce. So businesses have to make sure that the customer is willing to pay for it. Sometimes, it makes business sense to sacrifice a little bit of quality to save on price.

Too little

This oatmeal is very cheap, but it's cold and watery. I'm not sure I'll get it again.

Taste: 5/10
Texture: 4/10
Price: $2.50

Too much

This oatmeal is delicious and very creamy, but it's too expensive!

Taste: 9/10
Texture: 9/10
Price: $8.00

Just right

This oatmeal is perfect! It's creamy, hot and affordable.

Taste: 8/10
Texture: 7/10
Price: $3.95

Quality products that don't last forever

If a product lasts forever, customers won't ever need to buy a new one. So businesses often produce things they know will eventually look out of date, break or be overtaken by new, better versions. This encourages customers to buy a new product a little sooner than necessary. It's known as **planned obsolescence**.

Production failure

If production isn't properly managed it can have terrible consequences. For example, the Aral Sea in Central Asia has mostly dried up because of intensive cotton production. The lack of water is bad for people, animals and businesses too. Without water it's hard to grow more cotton.

Who's responsible?

I needed a cotton T-shirt, so I bought a cheap one in a fashionable store.

Consumer

My company sells T-shirts made from Central Asian cotton because it's cheap, which is what our customers want.

Fashion business

There's huge demand from the global fashion industry for cheap cotton. If we didn't provide it, someone else would!

Cotton producer

Cotton is one of our main sources of revenue. It's really important we keep producing cotton, and lots of it!

Government official

It was the decisions of businesses, consumers *and* governments that led to the Aral Sea drying up. Fixing these kinds of problems is tricky, when so many different people and organizations are involved.

The challenge for businesses is to balance satisfying consumers at the same time as producing in a **sustainable** way. That means cutting down on waste and pollution, and using natural resources responsibly. Sustainable production means production that doesn't harm workers or communities.

Sustainable production

One way of producing sustainably is for a business to plan *all* the stages of a product's life cycle right from the start.

How can it be designed to generate the least waste and use the fewest resources?

Designing the product

Recycle? Collect and reuse materials to make a new product?

Disposing of the product

Sourcing Materials

Where from? What's the impact on the environment? On people?

The whole product life cycle

Using the product

Making the product

Who makes it? How? Is it dangerous?

Easy to repair and maintain? Does it use energy? How much?

Distributing the product

Packaging

How is it transported? How far? How much pollution does that create?

What kind? How much? How do you dispose of it?

For example, here's how this sustainable shampoo from *Lush*, a British cosmetics brand, compares to most other shampoos you can buy:

REAL EXAMPLE

Shampoo in a bottle

Lush shampoo bars

No packaging – so when the shampoo is finished, there's nothing to throw away.

Longer-lasting – the bar can do as many washes as three shampoo bottles.

Smaller – so fewer trucks are needed to transport it, which means less pollution.

More expensive – each bar costs more to make than the average bottle, so it sells at a higher price.

Chapter 6:
Growing the business

At the beginning, all a business needs to do is survive. But if it all goes well, it should start making a profit. The next step can be to use that profit to **grow** and make more money. Usually this means growing in every way: hiring more staff, making more things and moving to bigger offices.

Growing is risky as it can cost a lot, but being bigger has lots of advantages, such as getting better deals from suppliers and the power to set prices. And ultimately, bigger businesses tend to make the greatest profits.

Bigger is better

If your business is doing well, it can be tempting to change nothing and keep it the same size. But this means missing out on some of the advantages of being bigger...

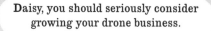
Daisy, you should seriously consider growing your drone business.

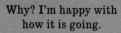
Why? I'm happy with how it is going.

Well, first of all, your costs will be lower. I've seen it firsthand with my hotel business.

Suppliers tend to give you better deals the more you buy.

Number of cartons	Price per carton
1	$3
10	$2.90
50	$2.75
100	$2.50

I pay less per carton than smaller hotels that only need 50 cartons.

Costs are spread more thinly when you produce more.

The hotel computer system costs the same for me as my smaller competitors. But I divide the cost between more bookings than they do.

And because each night's stay costs me less than it does my competitors...

... you can charge less than they do and still make a profit.

Exactly! And more guests will choose my hotel, because it's cheaper.

Mmm, maybe I should think about growing my business then!

It's often cheaper for a big business to do something than a small business. This is known as an **economy of scale**. So bigger businesses can set lower prices but still make a profit.

How to grow

Businesses can grow by producing more of the same thing or selling new products. This is known as growing **horizontally**. Or they can expand into *another* area of their supply chain, called growing **vertically**. To do this they may need more staff, a bigger building or more machinery – all of which cost money.

Towards suppliers

Towards customers

Vertically

Horizontally

My business makes drones. I then sell them to drone shops.

Daisy could buy the factory that produces drone parts. That way, Daisy would control the quality of the parts and get them more cheaply, too. She could also sell parts to other drone builders.

Daisy could expand her factory to make many more drones and benefit from economies of scale.

Daisy could try developing and selling new products, such as DIY drone kits, drone-flying courses or drone-flying events. This is known as **diversifying**.

Diversifying helps to reduce risk. Sales of one product might make up for falling sales of another.

Daisy could open her own drone shop, to sell her products directly to customers.

97

Catching a unicorn

Some new businesses grow extremely fast, reaching a value of a billion dollars in just a couple of years. These kind of businesses are so rare they are known as **unicorns**.

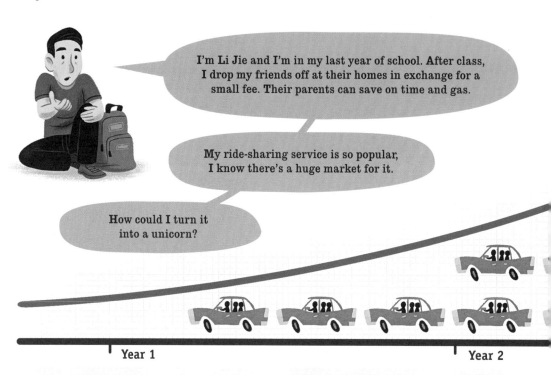

I'm Li Jie and I'm in my last year of school. After class, I drop my friends off at their homes in exchange for a small fee. Their parents can save on time and gas.

My ride-sharing service is so popular, I know there's a huge market for it.

How could I turn it into a unicorn?

Year 1

Year 2

Technology

Businesses that take advantage of new technologies can reach lots of customers quickly.

Instead of being a driver, why don't I connect *other* drivers with passengers? I'll build an app that allows people to book shared car rides.

Get funding

The more money you raise from investors, the lower you can push your prices. This helps win over customers and pushes competitors out of the market.

I think your app is going to be huge, Li Jie! My company will invest millions, which will pay for the app's expansion into cities around China.

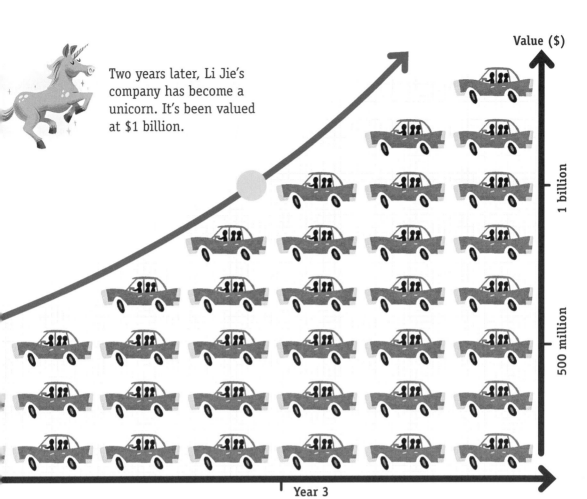

Two years later, Li Jie's company has become a unicorn. It's been valued at $1 billion.

Value ($)

1 billion

500 million

Year 3

Buy

A quick way to get lots more customers is to buy part of or all of a competitor's company.

Keep innovating

Even the most successful businesses need to keep evolving to stay on top of the competition.

Selling overseas

Selling to other countries is a good way of growing and reaching new customers. But what works in one place might not work elsewhere. To get it right, businesses need to research the new market. Will customers like the product? Where will they find it? Is it affordable?

For example, this book was written in the UK but is sold all around the world, sometimes in English but often in other languages. Here are some of the things the writers, designers and sales team had to think about:

The text might take up more space in other languages. Is there enough space?

Will people relate to these business examples in other countries?

REAL EXAMPLE

This price is in British Pounds (£). What should it cost in US dollars?

Are any of the images offensive in other cultures?

Does the diagram make sense if the text reads in another direction? For example, Arabic is read from right to left.

To have the best chance of success, a product needs to be tested on customers of the intended country and adapted accordingly.

Sometimes a product just won't work in another country. People may not want it if competitors in that country are already just as good.

Getting it there

It often takes a lot of time, money and paperwork to get products out of one country and into another. So after taking all those things into account, businesses need to decide if it's still worthwhile.

Floating the business

Businesses need to spend money in order to grow. One way to raise a *lot* of money is to allow anyone to buy shares in the business. This is known as **going public** or **floating on the stock market**. Once someone buys a share, they are called a **shareholder**.

Stock exchanges

Shares are sold to the public through marketplaces called **stock exchanges** ("stocks" has a similar meaning to "shares").

After buying shares in one business, a shareholder can later sell them on the stock exchange and buy shares in a different business.

This map shows the biggest stock exchanges around the world.

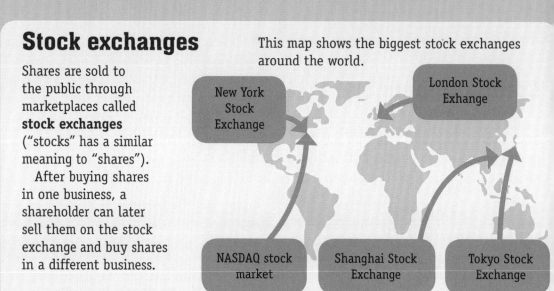

New York Stock Exchange

London Stock Exhange

NASDAQ stock market

Shanghai Stock Exchange

Tokyo Stock Exchange

Publicly owned businesses must have limited liability (see page 27). After going public, the business is called a **corporation**. Most of the world's biggest businesses have publicly owned shares:

$$$.com   Biggest 10 companies in 2017 by revenue:

1. Walmart, USA - retail
2. State Grid, China - energy
3. Sinopec Group, China - energy
4. China National Petroleum, China - energy
5. Toyota Motor, Japan - cars
6. Volkswagen, Germany - cars
7. Royal Dutch Shell, Netherlands - energy
8. Berkshire Hathaway, USA - finance
9. Apple, USA - technology
10. Exxon Mobil, USA - energy

★ Businesses with publicly owned shares

But floating in itself doesn't *make* a business huge. A business has to reach a decent size and stability before many people will *want* to buy shares.

To float or not to float?

Once a business goes public, it must share more information about itself. These are some of the things that it has to do.

Reveal any plans to be taken over by another business.	Announce new product launches in advance.	Report profits or losses several times a year.

It can help a business's competitors to know this information, which is a downside of being publicly owned. So even very large businesses may choose not to float.

What's the business worth?

When a business goes public, anyone can check its **share price** on the internet. If lots of people want to buy shares in the business, the price goes up. It goes down if lots of people want to sell their shares.

Share price is used as a signal of how well a company is doing. When share prices go up, it's good for the business.

Good publicity

Easier to attract private investors

Increased public profile, which can lead to increased product sales

 Easier to get loans from banks

But if share prices drop, the opposite is true.

Shareholders don't like it when share prices fall. If they are very unhappy, they can use their power to demand a change of management. So it becomes a priority for managers to keep shareholders happy.

Scandal

If a business is hit by scandal, share prices often fall. For example, when news broke in 2018 that *Facebook* users' data had been sold, *Facebook* share prices plummeted. Then *Facebook* had to deal with the reputational damage from *both* the scandal *and* the fall in share price.

THE DAILY

DATA FROM 80 MILLION FACEBOOK USERS SOLD

THE DAILY

FACEBOOK SHARE PRICE AT 6-YEAR LOW!!!

Too big to run?

There are disadvantages to being bigger, too. Eventually the size of a company makes it harder to keep track of everything. For example, here are some of the problems.

It's difficult to communicate effectively with thousands of employees.

When a company gets bigger it's harder to control waste.

People can feel unappreciated and isolated when they work for a huge company, so they become less productive.

Coordinating hundreds of suppliers is tricky too.

Too big to be fair?

A company can grow so big that it becomes the *only* supplier of a product. This is known as a **monopoly**. The problem with monopolies is the amount of power they have. For example, a milk distribution monopoly could decide to charge high prices to all customers. They could also pay dairy farmers a very low price.

So most governments make laws against monopolies being formed.

Is growth worth it?

Growing a business takes money, time and effort. So entrepreneurs need to weigh up whether the extra money or satisfaction they expect is worth it.

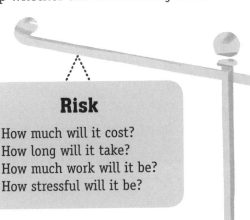

Risk

How much will it cost?
How long will it take?
How much work will it be?
How stressful will it be?

Reward

How much extra money will you make?
In one month? In one year?
Will it bring you satisfaction?

Some entrepreneurs don't want to change their lifestyle, so they decide not to grow their business – and that's ok too.

Too big to fail

When a company is *really big*, lots of people, and even other businesses, depend on it for jobs and revenue. So if the company looks as if it's about to fail, the government might decide to lend it money to prevent jobs from being lost and other businesses from failing too.

For example, if a bank, Bank A, runs out of money and collapses...

Its customers will lose the money in their bank accounts.

My business lost all its money so I've had to shut it down.

The business I work for shut, so I lost my job.

More people will lose their jobs and savings and won't be able to repay their loans to other banks.

More businesses will shut down...

I've lost all my money so I can't repay the money we borrowed from Bank B to buy our house.

Aaah, we have to stop this vicious spiral!

Eventually, Bank B will run out of money completely, and collapse.

We've heard Bank B's running out of money, so we're lining up to take our money out before it runs out.

With people not repaying their loans, Bank B will start to run out of money.

Banking crisis

In 2008, lots of American and European banks looked as if they were about to collapse after taking huge risks and losing lots of money. Several national governments decided to step in to prevent a spiral.

Many people protested against the decision to save the banks with public money.

Was it worth it?

Banks – and customers' accounts – were saved, but many countries still went into **recession** – a period when businesses sell less, lots of people are out of work and the country as a whole is poorer. Many people think it would have been even worse if the government had done nothing.

To try to prevent a banking crisis from happening again, governments have made banking rules stricter, to stop reckless risk-taking.

Chapter 7:
The bigger picture

By now, you'll know lots about how businesses work. But the chances of a business being successful may depend on many things you can't control: the **economy**, the **government**, even the weather.

This chapter explores some of those factors and how businesses can adapt to them.

How easy is it to do business?

Setting up and doing business is different in every country. In some places it takes longer to get things done. In others it might cost more – and sometimes it's not even possible to do business freely at all.

Here are some of the things that make doing business *easier*.

Infrastructure

Things such as roads, electric cables and schools are together known as **infrastructure.** Without them, businesses couldn't distribute products around a country, connect to the internet or employ skilled workers. Usually, infrastructure is taken care of by government and paid for by taxes (see page 58).

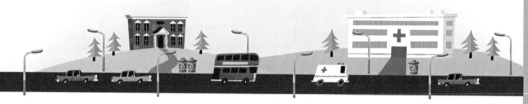

Property rights

If businesses don't have the right to own stuff, usually called **property rights**, it's difficult for them to compete fairly. This includes their goods but also their ideas.

Most countries have laws to stop inventions and ideas from being stolen, copied or sold without permission.

Here are some of the things that make doing business *harder*.

Corruption

Business people and politicians sometimes act dishonestly in order to gain power or money for themselves. This is called **corruption**. It gives an unfair advantage to some businesses over others, so governments make rules to stamp it out. Corruption can take many forms. Here are just a few.

Using threats or violence against a business, for example to shut a competitor down, is called **extortion**.

When a government official is also a business person, this creates something called a **conflict of interest**.

Hmmm! A new railway station is opening in 2025. I'll open a branch of my business right next door.

Asking for money in exchange for special treatment, such as processing an application quickly, is called **bribery**.

Red tape

Government rules can stop businesses from cheating customers. But excessive rules and regulations slow businesses down – because it makes them spend so much time filling out forms and getting permissions. This is known as **red tape**.

The role of government

In many countries, businesses don't have to worry about simple things such as infrastructure or property rights. That's because the government is working behind the scenes to make doing business *easier*. But sometimes the government can actually make doing business *harder*, by insisting on red tape.

The government's attitude to business – whether they tend to help or hinder – can affect how some people decide to vote in an election.

Supply and demand

Businesses thrive or fail based on their ability to make money. How much a business sells depends on how much it makes available to customers (**supply**) and how much customers are willing to buy (**demand**). In turn, supply and demand affect prices, like this.

Trisha's Flowers

If supply is low, businesses can charge lots.

Limited edition rare orchids: $25

$10 lilies - Popular for Mother's Day

If demand is high, businesses can charge lots, too.

If supply is high, businesses need to charge less to sell their supply.

If demand is low, businesses have to charge less to tempt customers.

In season bulbs $1.99 each

Mid-bloom flowers half price! $2.99 each

Managing supply and demand is tricky, because lots of things are constantly affecting them. Here are some examples Trisha has to deal with.

Weather
Frost can kill flowers, reducing the supply.

I always try to predict changes to supply and demand. I constantly adjust what I stock and how much I charge for everything.

Trends
There is increased demand for flowers that are in fashion, for example if a celebrity is pictured with them.

$2.99
50¢
$1.99

Competition
When a competitor lowers their prices, Trisha's become more expensive in comparison. So demand for her flowers goes down.

Price of fuel
If gas gets more expensive, Trisha has to raise the price of delivery. This in turn reduces demand.

Strong and weak economies

The **economy** of a country is made up of all the things people make, sell and buy from each other. Whether the economy is doing well or doing badly has a big effect on supply and demand for any individual business, too.

If people are making, buying and selling lots, the economy is said to be doing well.

BUY BUY SELL SELL

People have jobs and money to spend...

People feel confident about the future...

My pay will probably increase this year!

...so typically customers spend more.

If people are making, buying and selling less, the economy is said to be doing badly.

There's less to do, so fewer people are employed. People have less money to spend...

The future looks uncertain...

I should save my money in case the economy gets even worse.

...so usually customers spend less.

Recession

If the economy does badly for more than six months, it's known as a **recession**. Not every business will do badly – supermarkets selling at cheap prices might even do better. Governments and national banks try to prevent recessions, and bring countries out of recession.

Fixing business

A community can be home to bad businesses. In some cases, the problem sorts itself out:

A fall in demand sends a signal to a business, which can encourage them to improve. But often it's not that simple – and the government might need to intervene.

If a problem doesn't affect the consumers of a product, demand and supply can't fix it. This is known as **market failure**. So the government has to step in. For example, they might force a nightclub to move away from people's homes.

Sometimes the government steps in to encourage businesses to produce things that are *good* for consumers or society.

Wind farms provide clean sources of energy, but they're expensive to set up. So the government is giving grants to entrepreneurs building wind farms.

Government toolkit

Pollution is another example of market failure. Suppliers and consumers of goods and services that cause pollution don't suffer individually – but society does. As well as setting laws, here are some of the tools governments can use to tackle it.

Tax incentives

Governments can put a tax on cars that use lots of gasoline. By making them more expensive, it discourages people from buying those cars.

On the other hand, by reducing taxes on electric cars, the government can encourage people to switch to less polluting cars.

Ownership

Nobody "owns" rivers, so people don't always take care of them.

The government can give an institution, such as an environment agency, the power to act as if it owns the rivers. This means it's *their* responsibility to police rivers and fine polluters.

Information

Consumers don't always have enough information to know which products cause more harm than others.

I wonder which fruit is more ecofriendly?

To help, a government can force producers to put more information on a product label, such as the distance the product has traveled.

Worldwide agreements

Pollution is a worldwide problem – it doesn't stop at a country's border. What's more, polluting businesses sometimes operate in more than one country. So to tackle the problem, governments from around the world have to work together – but it's not always easy to agree.

Do we all agree that rich countries, which are the biggest polluters, should cut their pollution down most?

That's unfair! Rich countries still need factories to keep their economies going – even if they cause pollution. *Everyone* should cut down *the same.*

Poorer countries should be allowed to keep their factories, to help pull them out of poverty.

Aaaargh!

The cost of money

Businesses and consumers often need to borrow money from banks.
They have to *pay* to borrow money, because banks are businesses
too, and money-lending is one of their services. The price to borrow
money is called **interest**. The amount of interest is called the
interest rate – and, just like other prices, it changes all the time.

We're developing a technology to grow diamonds in a lab.

We need to borrow $100,000 to get our business started.

Citybank agrees to lend the business
$100,000, at a current interest rate of 10%.

10% of
$100,000 is
$10,000

$100,000

So *Diamond & Sons* will have to repay
$100,000 plus an extra $10,000, which
is **$110,000**.

The business has decided to repay the amount in chunks of $1,000 per month.

$1,000	$1,000	$1,000	$1,000	$1,000	$1,000	$1,000	$1,000	$1,000	$1,000
$1,000	$1,000	$1,000	$1,000	$1,000	$1,000	$1,000	$1,000	$1,000	$1,000
$1,000	$1,000	$1,000	$1,000	$1,000	$1,000	$1,000	$1,000	$1,000	$1,000
$1,000	$1,000	$1,000	$1,000	$1,000	$1,000	$1,000	$1,000	$1,000	$1,000
$1,000	$1,000	$1,000	$1,000	$1,000	$1,000	$1,000			
$1,000	$1,000	$1,000	$1,000	$1,000	$1,000	$1,000			
$1,000	$1,000	$1,000	$1,000	$1,000	$1,000	$1,000			
$1,000	$1,000	$1,000	$1,000	$1,000	$1,000	$1,000	$1,000	$1,000	$1,000
$1,000	$1,000	$1,000	$1,000	$1,000	$1,000	$1,000	$1,000		$1,0
$1,000	$1,000	$1,000	$1,000	$1,000	$1,000	$1,000	$1,000		$1,0
$1,000	$1,000	$1,000	$1,000	$1,000	$1,000	$1,000	$1,000		1,0

Eek! It's going to take us
110 months, or about 9
years to pay it all back.

🔲 loan   🔲 interest   TOTAL = $110,000

When interest rates change

In many countries, a national or central bank is in charge of the central interest rate. It's typical for the bank to raise or lower the rate a few times each year. Other banks who have borrowed from the central bank usually adjust their rates, too.

THE DAILY

Massive rise in interest rates

Businesses

The interest rate has increased from 10% to 17%. So now we have to repay $1,700 per month.

We'll have to find a way of making savings...

Why don't we move to a smaller lab so we pay less rent?

Consumers

Consumers also borrow from banks to buy big things, such as houses or cars. So when interest rates rise, their repayments go up. To save money, they might have to cut back on expensive or non-essential things...

Luxury handbags

Vacations

New cars

So, businesses selling luxuries can lose customers when interest rates go up.

Governments and central banks don't change interest rates just for fun. They are trying to keep a good economy strong, or to recover from a weak economy (see page 113).

It's a good idea for all businesses to follow the news about anything that will affect them in the near future, especially changes to interest rates.

The power of technology

Breakthroughs in science lead to new technologies, then new products and even new ways of doing business. Here's an example.

DNA and data

DNA is a part of your body that contains a coded "instruction manual" for how your body builds itself. Scientists have found cheap ways of reading an individual's DNA code, which has created all sorts of business opportunities...

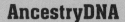

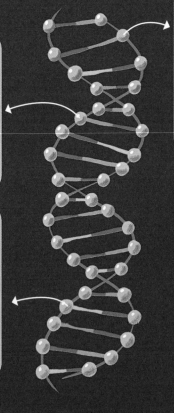

REAL EXAMPLES

DNAFit

This business promises to improve customers' diet and fitness based on their DNA profile.

23andMe

By analyzing their customers' DNA, this business can warn them if they are at risk of some particular diseases.

AncestryDNA

This business reveals customers' unknown relatives, and where distant ancestors came from, just by looking at their DNA.

With permission from their customers, these businesses can share their findings with DNA researchers. This could lead to more scientific breakthroughs, and more business opportunities.

Technology challenges

New technology often presents big questions for society. For instance, if the technology exists, should parents be allowed to change their child's DNA to make them more intelligent or beautiful?

Rise of the machines

When machines do tasks that humans used to do, or that humans can't do, it's known as **automation**. Businesses that invest in automation can often employ fewer people and lower their costs. That's because unlike employees, machines don't need salaries, time off or pensions.

This pizza business has automated its production process to make it...

...cheaper,

This software costs less than employing someone to take orders over the phone.

...quicker,

...and more reliable.

As a result, human employees lost their jobs. When this happens, businesses and governments need to help people retrain and find a new job.

But automation doesn't just destroy jobs, it can create them too.

I designed the software the pizza business uses to take orders.

I fix and maintain the pizza-making robotic arm.

And often machines only take on *certain tasks* rather than *whole jobs*.

ATM

I just dispense money.

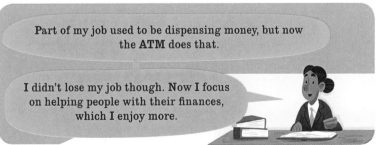

Part of my job used to be dispensing money, but now the **ATM** does that.

I didn't lose my job though. Now I focus on helping people with their finances, which I enjoy more.

Nobody knows for sure if increased automation technology will lead to fewer jobs overall. Currently people are still better than machines at all sorts of things – from writing a song, defending a victim in a court of law or building personal relations with customers, to fiddly jobs such as stacking books onto a shelf.

What now?

By now, you will understand what a business is, and how businesses fit into the world.

You may be a more shrewd customer, able to spot tricks that businesses use.

> The deluxe option is ridiculously expensive – this must be decoy pricing.

PEARL'S PCs

Basic	Standard	Deluxe
$500	$800	$2000

You might have ideas about how to encourage businesses to be more ethical.

> I'm only going to buy these if the business can guarantee the workers were paid a decent wage.

You will have the basic information you need to start your own business, if that's what you want to do. If you are feeling nervous, remember these things:

You don't need to have any particular personality to run a business. You only need to *want* to run a business.

> I'm quite shy, but I was so determined to make money that I made my business work.

You don't need to know *everything* about running a business before you start, and you don't need any formal qualifications.

> I started my app company when I was 14 and learned how to run a business just by doing it!

You can use things you've learned from being a customer. Copy things that you liked, and avoid anything that put you off.

> Ugggghhh...I hate it when a business sends too many emails!

Inbox — READ ME
Sent — Urgent
Drafts — Last chance!!!
Outbox — Jacob, don't delay
Folders — SPECIAL OFFER
Work — Hot deals NOW
— Best ever

You don't have to take huge risks. You can start modestly, test your ideas and plan realistically.

When I realized my magazine wasn't making money, I cut my costs to make the business work.

It doesn't matter if the first business you try doesn't work out. You can learn from what went wrong. Remember Thomas Edison, from page 62?

I failed with lots of business ideas, but I struck it big with my lightbulb!

If you want to start your own business, you could start with some of these activities:

Join a program that offers support and training to young people interested in business. These are often called Business Achievement Programs. Ask if there is one at your school or college, or search online for one in your local area or region.

Look for bargains in second-hand stores, then try selling them on for a profit.

Sell to your friends and family.

Make something simple and sell it. It could be keyrings, or earrings – or anything!

Rent a stall at a market.

Get to know local business people and chat with them about how they run their businesses.

Open a shop on an online marketplace such as *eBay* or *Etsy*.

Read the business section of newspapers, to learn more about why some businesses work and some don't.

Glossary

This glossary explains some of the words used in this book. Words written in *italic* type are explained in other entries.

accountant a professional that businesses pay to check the accuracy of their *accounts*.

accounts records of a business's *costs* and *revenues*.

advertising telling people about a product, for example on TV or a poster. Usually the business pays for this type of *promotion*.

bankruptcy when a person is unable to pay their debts, and his or her possessions are sold off to pay back *creditors*.

Board of Directors a team of experienced people who oversee the running of a business and *hire* and *fire* the *CEO*.

brand the identity of a business, displayed through everything from its name to its packaging materials.

business plan a document that describes a business in detail, usually with the aim of raising money from *investors*.

cash flow money that goes in and out of a business regularly.

CEO short for Chief Executive Officer, the most senior person in charge of running the business day-to-day. Sometimes called an MD, or Managing Director.

competition a rival business that might attract *customers* away from you.

consumer a person who uses *goods* or *services* – not always the same as a *customer*.

corporation a business that has *limited liability*, and trades *shares* on a stock market.

costs money a business spends before it can sell a *good* or *service*.

creditor a person or business that *loans* money to another business.

customer anyone who buys a *product*, even if they don't use it themselves.

data information, especially about people and the things they spend money on. Some businesses provide *services* in exchange for data rather than money.

diversity a range of different backgrounds and perspectives.

efficiency making a high quality product quickly and cheaply.

employee someone who works for a business, but is not in charge.

entrepreneur someone who runs their own business, or is starting up their own business.

ethical business any business that puts time and money into protecting the local community or environment.

exporting sending goods or services to another country to sell them.

firing when a *manager* tells an *employee* that they can't work for that business any longer.

franchise a new business that pays an existing business to use their business model.

funding money needed to start or grow a business.

good a physical thing that a business makes and/or sells.

grant money given to a business that doesn't have to be paid back.

growth when a business gets bigger, for example *producing* more and employing more people.

hiring when a business employs someone new.

importing bringing *goods* from another country to sell in your own country.

interest extra money you have to pay back to someone you have borrowed money from.

interest rate the proportion of a *loan* that is charged as *interest*.

investing putting money into a business, hoping to make a *profit* later.

investor a person, business or organization that invests in a business.

labor union an organization that supports *employees* to demand better working conditions from their employer.

liability the responsibility a business has to pay back any money it owes to its *creditors*.

limited liability only the business is responsible for paying back money, not its owners.

unlimited liability the business owners are personally responsible for paying back any money it owes.

liquidation selling off the possessions of a failed business, in order to pay back *creditors*.

LLC short for Limited Liability Company

loan money given to a business that has to be paid back.

manager an *employee* within a business who is in charge of other employees.

market the potential *customers* that may buy a business's *products*.

market research finding out what your *market* actually wants or doesn't want.

marketing ways that a business persuades people to buy its products, for example through clever *pricing* and *promotion*.

markup the price increase when a business buys a *product* at one price, but sells it for a higher price.

MD see *CEO*

micro-business a very small business, with fewer than ten *employees*.

monopoly when a business is the only provider of a *good* or *service*.

PR when a business influences what the public hears about it, for example by getting coverage on TV. Short for "public relations".

pricing deciding what a *product* should cost.

product anything a business sells, whether it's a *good* or a *service*.

production the process of making *goods* and *services* to sell.

profit any money left over after a business subtracts its *costs* from its *revenue*.

promotion publicizing a business's *products* to encourage people to buy them.

public services things such as roads, provided for everybody by a government, and not by a business.

retailer a business that sells *goods* to *consumers*, for example a grocery store.

revenue money that a business receives from selling its *products*.

service an activity that people pay a business to do, such as cleaning.

shareholder someone who owns *shares* in a business, and can receive a portion of any *profits*.

shares parts of the business that are owned by different people.

sole proprietor a person who is the only owner of a business and can keep any *profits* but is *liable* for any losses.

startup a new business, including a business that may not have begun selling anything yet.

supply chain the set of businesses that one business relies on to produce *goods* and *services*.

sustainability when a business or group of businesses ensures that their *production* methods do not harm the environment.

taxes money that individuals and businesses pay to the government, to be spent on *public services*.

unicorn a *startup* with a value of more than one billion dollars.

wholesaler a business that sells large amounts of *goods*, usually to a *retailer*.

workers' rights rules about how *employees* should be treated, including the right to form a *labor union*.

Index

Usborne Quicklinks

For links to websites where you can find out more about how business works, with videos and activities, and tips on how to start your own business, go to the Usborne Quicklinks website at

www.usborne.com/quicklinks

and type in the title of this book. Please follow the internet safety guidelines at the Usborne Quicklinks website.

Here are some of the things you can do at Usborne Quicklinks:

Works on my cell phone, too!

- Play games and quizzes to test your business skills
- Meet young entrepreneurs who have started their own businesses
- Take a virtual tour of a factory
- See inside the New York Stock Exchange

Acknowledgements

Written by
Lara Bryan & Rose Hall

Illustrated by
Kellan Stover

Edited by
Alex Frith

American editor: Carrie Armstrong
Series editor: Jane Chisholm

Designed by Jamie Ball
& Freya Harrison

Series designer:
Stephen Moncrieff

Business experts:
Wilson Turkington &
Bryony Henry